In the Legion of th

IN THE LEGION OF THE VANGUARD

JOHN A. PINKMAN

Edited by
FRANCIS E. MAGUIRE

MERCIER PRESS

IRISH AMERICAN BOOK COMPANY (IABC)
Boulder, Colorado

MERCIER PRESS
PO Box 5, 5 French Church Street, Cork
16 Hume Street, Dublin 2

Trade enquiries to CMD DISTRIBUTION,
55a Spruce Avenue, Stillorgan Industrial Park, Blackrock, Dublin

Published in the US and Canada by the
IRISH AMERICAN BOOK COMPANY
6309 Monarch Park Place, Niwot, Colorado, 80503
Tel: (303) 652 2710, (800) 452-7115
Fax: (303) 652 2689, (800) 401-9705

ISBN 1 85635 233 1
10 9 8 7 6 5 4 3 2 1

DEDICATED TO
SEAN ÓG

Printed in Ireland by Colour Books Ltd.

PUBLISHER'S NOTE

In the Legion of the Vanguard is one participant's account of particular episodes in the War of Independence and the Civil War and his own part in them. John Pinkman's opinions are forthright and have a ring of honesty and authenticity. In some cases, however, it has not been possible to corroborate his testimony, which at times contradicts in important details accounts of the period by historians. The book is presented as a significant primary historical document and an important contribution to our understanding of the events of the War of Independence and the Civil War.

PREFACE

John Pinkman tells of his childhood and youth in a closely knit, strongly nationalistic Irish Catholic community in Liverpool's dockland. Subjected at an early age to the anti-Catholic and anti-Irish discrimination characteristic of that time and place, he joined a Sinn Féin club at the age of sixteen years and then the Liverpool Company of the Irish Volunteers (Old IRA) two years later. Arrested and sentenced to five years' penal servitude in Dartmoor Prison for 'Sinn Féin activities', he describes the brutal life he and others endured in England's most dreaded prison.

On his release from Dartmoor Prison (following the Anglo-Irish Treaty), he joined the elite Dublin Guards Brigade of the Irish National Army on its formation early in 1922. Soon caught up in the vicious fighting of the Civil War, he provides an eyewitness account of the major events in that war in Kilkenny, Dublin and in Munster.

John was one of several Old IRA veterans I interviewed in Dublin in the mid-1960s while researching material for a thesis on the Liverpool Company of the Irish Volunteers. Our experiences of New York, Liverpool and the west of Ireland enhanced the rapport between us. Impressed by both his unusually adventurous life and his remarkable memory for detail, I encouraged him to write an account of his extraordinary life offering to assist him in preparing the manuscript for publication. After his death in March, 1970 I obtained his handwritten drafts and began preparing his material for publication.

In the Legion of the Vanguard focuses on his activity as a Volunteer in the Liverpool Company during the War of Independence and as a soldier of the Dublin Guards Brigade during the Civil War.

As we commemorate the seventy-fifth anniversary of the ending of that war, it is timely to read an eye-witness account by a participant who describes with candour, honesty and occasional humour what happened in some of the key events of the war.

FRANCIS E. MAGUIRE

1

I WAS BORN IN BOOTLE, Liverpool on 3 January 1902, the second youngest of the six children in our family of four girls and two boys. Both my parents came from the west of Ireland. My father, Francis, was born on 1 November 1854 on his father's farm in the townland of Mullaghboy, Kilclare, Co. Leitrim. As the youngest son in a family of seven children he had no prospect of inheriting his father's farm, and like so many of the younger sons in the west of Ireland, he left the farm as a young man. He became an apprenticed painter in Dublin, but found that even tradesmen starved there, so he sailed for England and settled in Liverpool. My mother, Catherine McSherry, came from a small farm in Glenade in the north of Co. Leitrim.

Our family name, Pinkman, is rare. Originally *Mag Uidhir,*[1] it was translated – or mistranslated – in the wake of the Williamite land confiscations of 1691-1703 by an English landlord's agent who was responsible for giving much the same treatment to a neighbouring family of Ó Gormfhlaithigh[2] whose name he rendered into Blueman. Despite our English surname, however, we are descended from the Maguires of Fermanagh.

I always remember my father as the finest man I ever knew. He was quiet and dignified, with eyes that were firm but never severe, and he wore a neatly trimmed beard. A strict parent, he watched over us like a hawk and paid particular attention to the companions we played with. A deeply religious man, he attended mass every morning of his life. But he never spoke about religion, he never preached it. We never heard him saying his prayers, or quoting the bible, or anything like that. That was the most beautiful thing about him: he was such a deeply religious man, yet he never paraded his beliefs.

My mother – Lord have Mercy on her – was a great, big, warm-hearted Irish mother. She was full of the old Irish customs and pishogues, such as taking a new-laid egg and making the sign of the cross with it – in Irish – over my eyes, for protection against blindness.

Our home was an Irish home. My mother and father were Irish

speakers and often talked to each other in Irish when they had something to say to each other that they didn't want us children to hear. Their friends who came to visit were always Irish friends from the west. If you wanted to sing a song in our house, you always sang an Irish song. The music and the dances were Irish: with my brother Frank on the violin and my sisters on the piano, there'd be jigs and reels at the drop of a hat. Someone would call for *The Old Plaid Shawl,* then for *The Irish Washerwoman* or *The Connaughtman's Ramble.* Even the whiskey was Irish! When the Connaught crowd came in, the bottle of O'Donovan's Irish whiskey was brought out. If we sat down to cards, we played Irish card games, such as twenty-five. On the walls were pictures of some of the old Fenians; there was a large framed engraving of Parnell which was my father's pride and joy. In the bedrooms there were picture scenes of Ireland; the Shrine at Knock was the one in my bedroom.

Every summer we went to Ireland for our holidays. My mother would take us to Dublin on the cross-channel boat, and then by train to Sligo where Uncle Mike Foley would meet us with his horse and trap and take us to his home in Castlegal near Mullaghmore. There we met our cousins, and each year I looked forward to seeing my favourite cousin, Bernie Meehan. From Castlegal and Creevykeel we often went on foot to Drumacolla, Glenade to another uncle, Dan McSherry. We used to play among the hay in his fields and meadows, and it was there that we met the Rooney girls from the neighbouring farm in the townland of Drumcashel. Pat Rooney had six daughters: Bea, Molly, Kate, Margaret, Tessie, and Annie – and I fell in love with Annie.

I was always heartbroken when those wonderful, unforgettable holidays came to an end and it was time to return to the smoke and grime of Liverpool. But we always brought back with us great baskets of home-cured bacon and ham, and pounds of fresh butter. We never forgot to take home with us a couple of good, fat chickens – and a big bundle of *crannagh* or *duileasc* [edible seaweed].

We lived in St James' parish and when I was old enough, I went to St James' Elementary School. When I reached Standard Four, however, my mother sent me to St James' Select School because she didn't like the Standard Four teacher. The Select School was for the kids of the better-off families who didn't want their sons and daughters mixing with the common herd – the lower orders – and were able to pay the sixpence-a-week school fee. The Elementary School was free, and many of the boys and girls going there were terribly poor; some of them were given a free breakfast – a mug of cocoa and a slice of bread – free corduroys, and free clogs. The clogs were big wooden ones with iron clickers.

At the Select School all the children were well-dressed – the boys wore white celluloid collars – and everyone had proper shoes. At the end of my year there, I returned to St James' Elementary School and started Standard Five.

Our teacher in Standard Five was a Mr O'Connor who was great on religion and did everything he could to encourage us to go to daily mass. On the wall he had a big sheet of paper with a list of all our names on it, and every time we went to mass he put a black cross against our name, and if we went to communion we got a red mark.

The brightest pupil in the room was a lad named Mooney: he always got his sums right and was top of the class. And he had more red crosses against his name than anyone else. 'If you were only like Mooney,' O'Connor would say to us, 'and went to communion every morning, you'd get all your sums right, too.'

He was very proud of Mooney whom he held up as an example to the rest of us, and singled out for the priests who often called into the class on visits. One day Fr Casey came in and when Mooney's outstanding academic and spiritual records were pointed out, the priest asked Mooney if he'd seen Fr Mulligan on the altar that morning. Mooney suddenly became very confused, and stammered that he didn't know, and O'Connor got suspicious. O'Connor went to mass every morning for the next week and discovered that Mooney never put his foot inside the door of the church. It nearly broke O'Connor's heart when he saw he'd been made a fool of. He became a changed man. He never trusted us after that.

When I reached Standard Seven – the last year of the school – we had a lady drawing teacher, the only lady allowed to teach the boys in Standard Seven. I was fourteen years old then. I remember her very well because one day she accused me of stealing a pencil. That day she told us to draw a picture of what we wanted to be when we left school. If we wanted to be a fireman, we could draw a picture of a fireman climbing up a ladder to a burning house, or if we wanted to be a jockey, we could draw a jockey riding a horse in a race, and so on. I thought I'd like to be a monk – I was an altar boy then – so I drew a picture of a monk praying in his cell. When I'd finished the drawing I was playing with my pencil; other kids might bite their pencils, but I had the habit of scratching my ankle with mine. The next thing, some boy shot up his hand and cried out, 'Please Miss! Johnny's stealing a pencil!'

The teacher asked me what I was doing and I showed her. She called me out to the front of the class, hit me a galer [a strong blow] across the head, and looked at the picture I'd drawn.

'And this boy is going to be a monk!' she said, holding up my drawing for everyone to see. I went scarlet. I felt so ashamed. She'd made such an awful show of me in front of all the others.

But that was nothing compared to what happened to little Paddy McKenna. Paddy had a fine singing voice; he took private singing lessons after school and sang at high mass on Sundays. One day a teacher mimicked him during class and Paddy was never able to sing a note afterwards. The teachers there hadn't a clue. Most of them weren't properly trained teachers at all – the parish priest simply appointed whomever he wished.

The school-leaving age was fourteen then and I turned fourteen in January, 1916 while in Standard Seven – the final class of Elementary School. I had started thinking of what I was going to do when I left school at the end of the term; I'd changed my mind about being a monk! My parents advised me to go in for the engineering trade – to become an apprenticed fitter and turner. This meant I would have to attend the Bootle Junior Day Technical School – near the Bootle Town Hall – for two years before I could begin my engineering apprenticeship at sixteen.

Each year there were about thirty places in the Technical School open to the lads in the Borough of Bootle, and the competition to get in was terrific. To enter the Tech a boy had to pass an entrance examination – a few free places being given to those lads with the highest marks. If it was hard enough for non-Catholic lads to get in, it was far worse for us because only about three Catholic lads were taken each year. Those were the days when job advertisements in the English newspapers – particularly the Liverpool papers – said: 'No Catholics need apply' or 'No Irish wanted'. Religious discrimination was frequent and vicious. Catholics, especially Irish Catholics, were treated like dirt.

A couple of days before the entrance examination was to be held, my mother told me to tell my teacher that I wanted my name put down for the test, even though I wasn't in 'X7' – the special bench in our class for the four or five boys being specially prepared for the examination. The next day I put my hand up in class and told the teacher that I wanted to go in for the examination, so he called me out to the front. 'Look at this ass!' he said 'Just look at this ass who wants to sit the examination tomorrow! Get back, donkey. Get back to your desk!'

When I got home and told my mother, she went wild. Giving the shilling examination fee to my older brother Frank, she told him to take me to the Technical School in the morning. She said I was to do the examination anyway, and that if I didn't win a free place she'd pay the shilling-a-week tuition fee if I passed.

Frank took me to the Technical School the next morning on his way to work – he worked as a clerk in the Medical Officer's department in the Town Hall. Soon after I arrived, the candidates were divided into two groups, A and B. When the results came out I was top of the B group and my mother went straight up to my teacher and wiped the floor with him. I was the only boy from St James' who got into the Bootle Junior Day Technical School that year.

I attended the Technical School for the next two years and took such subjects as geometry, machine-drawing, metal work, and English. There were three Catholic boys in the class, which was the usual number allowed in each year. One of them was called Hooter, and the other was a dark, swarthy boy from St Winifred's who died shortly after finishing the course.

One occasion stands out very clearly in my memory of those two years. It was on Empire Day. All the boys and the teachers were lined up on the playground which was covered with a reddish-coloured gravel and looked like a parade square. In the middle of one side of the yard stood a flag-pole with the Union Jack flying from the top. As I looked at it, all I could think of was the execution of the 1916 leaders in Dublin. Each boy – one at a time – had to cross the yard, salute the flag, and join his classmates on the other side. When it came to my turn, I walked straight past the flag without saluting. I was the only boy in the entire school who didn't salute the Union Jack. I *wouldn't* salute it! All the teachers were there, lined up watching us, but not a word was said to me.

One teacher at that school I'll never forget was a Mr Jones who lived not far from me. For some bit of schoolboy's devilment I did one day, Mr Jones told me to stay in after school and write out two hundred lines. 'Any line you like,' he said. 'Write your own line.'

The Great War was on, and I sat down and wrote: 'Your King and Country need you' – two hundred times. In the morning, I handed in my lines; he looked at them, went white as death, and walked out of the room. He never spoke to me after that, except when absolutely necessary. I had done a terribly cruel thing – a schoolboy's thoughtlessly cruel taunt – and I've regretted it ever since. He was the only support of a large family whose father, the verger at St Leonard's Anglican church, was going blind.

When my two years at the Technical School ended – I was sixteen then – I had to choose a firm at which to do my engineering apprenticeship. I considered Harland & Wolff's, which was one of the best-known names in marine engineering on Merseyside. Most of the other lads' parents urged their sons to apply to Harland & Wolff's, but my mother told me to go to John Marsdens, and later I was glad I did. Harland & Wolff's was so big that an apprentice was usually put into one section and left there for most of the period of his apprenticeship; whereas at Marsdens, an apprentice spent some of his time in all the departments. The result was that Marsdens turned out the best and most versatile engineering fitters in Liverpool.

Shortly before I left the Technical School, the engineering instructor, an old marine engineer himself, asked each of us what his ambition was. I said to him 'To be chief engineer of the *Mauretania,* sir.' He looked straight down at me and shook his head slowly. 'That, boy, you can never be,' he said. He knew what I was up against because I was a Catholic.

I was glad enough when my two years ended at the Technical School. The few Catholic boys there – about six in the entire school – knew we weren't really welcome: we were there on sufferance as a concession to the Catholic population of Bootle.

I started my five-year apprenticeship at Marsdens in the summer of 1918. Work began at half-past seven in the morning and ended at five o'clock in the afternoon. We had an hour for dinner; there were no tea breaks – and there were no holidays either! I was paid two shillings and sixpence a week when I started, but this went up to twelve shillings and sixpence a week when I got the war bonus.

I really liked working at Marsdens and got on very well there. I'd always had a mechanical bent, and soon became pretty good at my trade. My best pal at Marsdens was another apprentice, Frank Robinson, who started serving his time the same day I did.

I had only just started serving my time when the men there pulled a couple of fast ones on myself and Green, another apprentice. We were sent up to the foreman of the iron foundry and told to ask him for the loan of his testicles. But the foreman said he didn't have any to lend us just then, but to go to Mr Reece in the brass foundry. Mr Reece sent us to Mr Rice in the copper shop, and from there we were sent from shop to shop until finally we got to the tin shop where one of the men said, 'Here, I think this is what you want. Get a handful of these!' – and he gave us some huge cast-iron links so heavy that we could hardly lift them. When we got them to the iron foundry, a fitter told us we were a pair of bloody eedjits; that what we had weren't testicles at all, but to go to the manager's secretary, Mrs so-and-so, and ask her for hers. When we did, she went livid with fury and screamed at us until we fled. I'm sure the story went through all the engineering shops in Liverpool.

As if that wasn't enough, a few weeks later one of the fitters I worked with came up to me and asked me to do him a favour at dinner-time – to step out to Blackledge's dairy and bring him back a pint of maiden's milk. When I asked the girl in the shop, she picked up a noggin measure, threw it at me and chased me out the door. After a couple of stunts like that the men generally left the apprentices alone.

There was one lad, an apprenticed tinsmith, a wild young lad who liked to shout and scream above the noise. One day he was working on the glazing machine and sat on the belt to take a ride for a few feet, but his foot stuck against a lever and he found himself hopelessly jammed in the machine while a metal ripper advanced and sheared his leg off. Everyone had heard his screams but thought he was just acting the clown.

The first ship I worked on was the battleship *Ramillies* which came into dry dock for repairs. I was delighted when I was sent down to work on her for overtime. It was my first real fitting job and we put cross-segments on the steering gear because vibration had loosened the bolts.

I started in the pattern-maker's shop at Marsdens, then went to the iron moulders and soon found myself in the tool stores. When a fitter wanted a five-eighths drill, we gave him one from the racks and he signed for it or gave in a tally. I had worked in the stores for only a few days when one of the fitters came up to the counter and got pretty nasty with me.

'What's your name?' he said. 'I hear you're an effin' Papist. Do you know what we do with Papists around here? We beat their effin' brains in.'

Every time he came up for a tool he cursed the Pope, the priests, the nuns – everything to do with the Catholic Church – until I was nearly in tears with rage. One day, I vowed, I'll kill the bastard.

The next time he came to the counter I grabbed a hammer. 'Now say it!' I said. 'Now say it, you Orange bastard.'

He looked down at me – he was a tall, well-built fellow. 'You can drop that hammer,' he said, starting to smile. 'Shake hands!' he said, offering me his hand. 'I'm a Catholic, too. I was only weighing you up – to see what you were made of.'

I always remembered that. His name was Packenham.

But I got along well with the men at Marsdens. Most of the foremen were Welsh, and many of the tradesmen were Welsh. We were always getting their names mixed up. There were two fellows, one was Owen Evans, and the other was Evan Owens.

Marsdens was at the bottom of Dacre Street, right on the boundary between the City of Liverpool and the Borough of Bootle. Next to us was the electrical engineering firm of Campbell & Isherwoods that did a lot of the electrical contracting at the docks. I knew some of the apprentices from Campbell & Isherwoods: one of them was a friend of mine, Charlie O'Gorman. At dinner-time we sometimes used to slip over the dock wall and steal oranges from the warehouses.

But neither Charlie nor I completed our apprenticeships. When I had only a year to go before getting my papers, both of us were arrested for IRA activity.

2

I WAS SIXTEEN WHEN I joined the Roger Casement Sinn Féin[3] club in Bridge Road, Litherland, a borough adjacent to Bootle in the north of Liverpool. The Sinn Féin club held its meetings in the premises of the Irish National Foresters' Society – a benevolent association – above a bicycle shop in Bridge Road.

It was natural for me to join the Sinn Féin club because I had grown up in such a strong Irish atmosphere at home. I loved Ireland and hated what British imperialism had done to Ireland and the Irish people. My father was born less than ten years after the Great Famine when nearly two million Irish people were allowed to die of starvation. Irish people were dying on the roadsides eating grass while grain was being shipped out of Dublin to pay rents to absentee English landlords. I'd read books on Irish history and learned of the cruelties suffered by the Irish people in the past, and I could see the sort of treatment they were getting in England in my own day.

The Irish Rising of 1916 had taken place only two years before I joined. My cousin Bernie Meehan from Sligo had been arrested for his part in the Rising and interned at Frongoch Camp in North Wales. My mother used to send him food parcels, and when he was released he stayed with us until my mother got him a job at John Hughes' store in Liverpool.

Bernie and I used to go to the ceilí dances held regularly at the Sinn Féin club, and after I had been going there for some months, Niall Lively and a couple of the lads told me one evening that there was some talk about forming a Volunteer company of the Irish Republican Army in Liverpool: a company on the same lines as those being formed in Ireland to fight for Irish freedom. I told them I was all for the idea, and that I'd join the company if it was started. They told me that they were thinking of starting one, and would let me know when they called the first meeting. At that time they were just trying to find out how many would be interested.

I attended the first meeting of the company which was held in

Bridge Road – in the same room where the Sinn Féin club met: I was seventeen at the time. There were about six or eight of us at that first meeting, and we just sat around on the benches and talked.

More than anyone, else Niall Lively, whose family lived near mine in Wordsworth Street, Bootle, was responsible for my joining the company. The Livelys were a very nationalistic Irish family from Cork. Niall's father – Patrick Lively – was a baker, and District Circle Head of the IRB[4] in Liverpool. Their home was a depot for munitions on their way across to Dublin. Niall's sister Moira was a great friend of my sister Kathleen, and I remember Niall's father bringing back from Dublin two sailors' hats for the girls with *Erin go Brath* on the ribbons. It was Niall's father who took Niall and me to see our first hurling game in Liverpool. Moira Lively became one of the most active members of the Cumann na mBan[5] in Liverpool.

The meetings of the company were held irregularly as a precaution against police raids. Tom Craven, who had taken part in the 1916 Rising, was our captain. He was a nice, quiet-spoken man, much like Patrick Pearse in appearance – with the same high brow. Usually there were eight or so of us – certainly never more than twelve – at those early meetings, and we sat around on the benches while Tom lectured us on the elements of street fighting. He told us how to barricade a room, how to protect ourselves from flying glass, and so on.

Then one summer's evening, as he sat quietly by the window during one of our meetings, Tom suddenly said: 'Boys, I'm going off to America!' without any explanation. We were shocked and disappointed, but we didn't ask any questions. We wondered how he could leave us: we didn't think it was right.

After he left, we elected Mike O'Leary as our new captain, and Tom Kerr as our lieutenant. (A couple of years ago I was surprised and amused when I read a front page article in *An tÓglach*[6] entitled: 'The Liverpool Battalion' by 'Iron Mike' O'Leary. I don't know when or how he earned the title 'Iron Mike,' but he certainly wasn't known to us as 'Iron Mike.') When Mike became our captain, we began to hold some of our meetings in the basement of No. 93 Scotland Road in Liverpool, and the lectures became increasingly political while the emphasis on street fighting and tactics declined. Many of us became disgruntled to see our company losing its military purpose, and our morale began to drop.

Seán Harrington – Lord have Mercy on him! – lived near our home in Bootle and we had been close friends for several years. His family came from Cork and he had a strong Cork accent. After one of our meetings in Scotland Road, he told me how disgusted he was with the way O'Leary was running the meetings of the company and that something had to be done, and I agreed with him. 'We've got to get rid of him,' he said, 'otherwise we'll have no company left. A lot of the men are losing interest and are leaving the Volunteers.'

I fully agreed with him – he'd taken the words right out of my mouth – so we decided to get O'Leary out and put in Tom Kerr as our new captain. We called for an election, and Tom was voted in as our new captain, and immediately the company reverted to its proper military role. (In his article in *An tÓglach* O'Leary put it very neatly that he summoned a meeting of the company, handed in his resignation, and returned to the ranks, suggesting that he decided to resign because he was unable to devote to his position the time and energy it required.)

The company took on a new life under Tom, but the man behind Tom was his father Neill Kerr who kept the Irish militant movement alive in Liverpool after the 1916 Rising. The Kerrs, originally from Armagh, lived in Florida Street, off Strand Road, in Bootle. Tom was a big, powerfully built man over six feet tall who worked as a docker. His father worked on the docks as a fitter's labourer. When the Irish Volunteers were being formed in Armagh, Tom Kerr – so I'm told – attended the first meeting and got up and demanded to know when they could start shooting the RIC![8] That was the sort of man Tom was; he was for action. He and his two brothers, Jack and Neill, had gone over to Dublin for the Rising and took part in the fighting at the General Post Office.

Tom taught us military drill, semaphore, and military tactics. He saw that we got copies of *An tÓglach*, the IRA military newspaper that was secretly published in Dublin and smuggled across to Liverpool.

He organised football games for the company and we played on the shore at Seaforth on Sunday afternoons. The football games were an ideal cover for our meetings because after we kicked the ball around for a while, we would sit on the sand far away from anyone else and hold a meeting of the company! But we were never able to field two full teams; that's how few we were – less than twenty-two members.

Tom organised a first-aid course for us so we'd know what to do if we got wounded. The course was given by a Jewish medical student from the Universtiy of Liverpool. Although he never got to know us personally, he talked to us about the structure of the body, about the bones, the veins and the arteries, the vital parts of the body, how to take care of a wound, and so on.

After one of our meetings, Tom told me he was going to make me a mobiliser for the company, meaning that I was to notify the men when a meeting was to be held. He said I was just the man for the job, because having grown up in Bootle, I knew Bootle, Kirkdale, Litherland and Seaforth like the back of my hand, and unlike most of the other fellows in the company, I spoke with a Liverpool accent. When a meeting was called, I'd slip around and tell the lads there was to be a meeting of the Irish Literary Society.

One evening I knocked on the door of an Irish boarding house where a couple of the lads lived but they happened to be out at the time, so I asked the landlady to tell the boys to be at a meeting of the Irish Literary Society at such-and-such a time. She was a big, hearty Irishwoman, and I can still see her standing in the doorway splitting her sides laughing at the idea of the two gobshites belonging to a literary society.

It was the general rule of the Liverpool Company that no one was admitted to our ranks unless he was personally known to at least one Volunteer who could vouch for the candidate's integrity. The rule was a sensible one, designed to preserve the security of the company and prevent it from being penetrated by spies and informers arriving in Liverpool among the large number of transient Irishmen coming over from Dublin. If there was ever any doubt about a prospective candidate – or any suspicion that he might be a renegade Volunteer from Ireland – we always sent him to see Mr Moran, the manager of the Irish National Foresters' head office in Liverpool. We would tell the fellow that in order to become a member of the Liverpool Company of the IRA, he would have to join the health benefit scheme which was the main feature of the Irish National Foresters. What the fellow didn't know was that when he handed his completed application form to Mr Moran's secretary, Nan Feeley, she made a copy of the applicant's name, birthplace, parents' names, etc., and then sent a copy to IRA Headquarters in Dublin. Michael Collins would then send the information to the IRA intelligence officer in the area from which the applicant hailed and ask for it to be verified. Only when we received from Dublin a satisfactory report on the fellow would we consider accepting him into the company.

It was a foolproof system, and never to my knowledge was the Liverpool Company infiltrated by British agents or informers. Much of the credit for the success of the system was due to Nan Feeley, a member of the Liverpool Cumann na mBan who married one of our volunteers, Jim McCaughey.

Sometimes we held our meetings at the Irish National Foresters' Hall in Bridge Road, Litherland, at other times we held them at No. 93 Scotland Road in the city of Liverpool, but I can never remember more than about thirty Volunteers at any meeting, and I attended all the meetings. In later years literally scores of men claimed to have belonged to the 'Liverpool Battalion,' or, God help us! the 'Liverpool Brigade' of the old IRA, and obtained medals and pensions from the Irish government in recognition of their 'service' in the fight for Irish independence. Some even wrote accounts of their 'exploits' in Liverpool for the gullible Irish newspapers. But there was never a battalion of the Old IRA in Liverpool: there was only one undermanned company – and because I was one of its two mobilisers, I knew every man who belonged to it.

The small group of us continued to train under Tom Kerr's leadership, but I was getting restless for action when I met a couple of Dublin lads, Joe Jackson and his brother Frank, who were boarders at Mrs Lively's house. Although neither Joe nor Frank attended any of our company's meetings, Joe came up to me one day and said it was a pity I spent all my time going to meetings and listening to a lot of talk when there were brave men in Ireland fighting day and night against the Black and Tans; that the Volunteers in Ireland were real soldiers but were handicapped because they didn't have enough guns and ammunition; and that it was a crying shame that the Liverpool Volunteers sat on their arses doing nothing to help them.

I thought he was right and asked him what I could do to help the fellows across in Dublin. He told me he knew a place in Liverpool where we could get bullets and revolvers, but not to let on to the others because they really didn't want any action – they only wanted to sit and talk. So I said I was game for anything he suggested because I *was* getting fed up with nothing but lectures.

He told me he had a friend, Joe Comerford, who would help us, but first we needed a couple of jemmies. I promised to get them and the next day at Marsdens I went up to one of the blacksmiths and asked him to make me a jemmy for a plug of tobacco, and he said he'd make me half a dozen. The blacksmith was a real old-timer who'd do anything for a plug or a pint. I told him to make me a couple and he made two of the finest steel jemmies I've ever seen. I took them to Joe who said they'd do just fine. He'd case the place where the guns were, and we'd meet with Comerford the following night at seven o'clock outside Lively's house.

We met at Lively's and took a tram from Rimrose Road up to Dale Street in Liverpool. To kill time until it was dark, we had a game of billiards and then went into a tea shop for a cup of tea. When it was dark enough, we walked along South Castle Street until we came to a gun shop in one of the old-fashioned buildings. Jackson and Comerford jemmied open the glass door, and leaving me to keep watch outside, went into the shop and filled their pockets with revolvers. When they had taken all they could carry, they called me inside and told me to grab all the ammunition I could get my hands on. There were boxes of the stuff all round me, and I dived into them with both hands and filled every pocket in my clothes, even those in my waistcoat. When I came out of the shop I was staggering under the weight of hundreds of bullets in my pockets.

Having left the shop, we crossed the street, cut through a lane, and took the first tram that came along. The tram was filled with people going to the theatre so we had to stand up in the centre of the tram as it lurched and rattled along on its rails.

The conductor made his way through the tram calling out: 'Fares please!' and I reached in my pocket for the money. Jasus! the sweat began to pour out of me as I fumbled in my pockets trying to find some coppers without letting the bullets tumble out. Luckily, Joe Jackson saw the fix I was in and he called out to me, 'It's all right, Johnny! I've got it!' and he gave the conductor a tanner and got three tuppenny tickets.

After a few stops, we got off that tramcar and took another one back to Scotland Road. But before we caught the next tram, I told Jackson to give me a couple of coppers because I couldn't get my hands in my pockets. The two of them looked at me and laughed their heads off. They were a cool pair of customers; typical Dublin jackeens, the two of them.

They decided we should go to old Peter Murphy's place – the '98 Shop – in Scotland Road, but Peter wasn't in, so we went down to No. 93, where the company sometimes met, but we couldn't get in there either so we took a tram back to Mrs Lively's. Mrs Lively was grinning from ear to ear when we got to her place, and she took us straight into the front parlour. 'Put them there, boys!' she said as she swept the cushions off the sofa. When we'd emptied out our pockets there were twelve revolvers lined up in a row, and hundreds of bullets of various calibre – mostly .32s and .38s.

'You'll be needing a cup of tea, boys, I suppose,' said Mrs Lively, and we all sat down and had a nice cup of tea while we admired the revolvers and ammunition.

'Take your pick, Seán!' said Comerford. 'You get first choice.' So I picked out a little nickel-plated .32

'Why did you take that one?' asked Comerford.

'Because it'll fit just nicely into my waistcoat pocket.' I said.

Then Comerford said they were going to Dublin the next night and he asked me if I wanted to go with them, and Mrs Lively said I should.

'We'll meet all the boys of the Dublin Brigade,' said Jackson, 'all Mick Collins' boys.'

I didn't know what to do. I wanted to join the Active Service Unit[9] but still had my apprencticeship to finish. To tell the truth, I was afraid of my mother and what she'd say to me if I told her I was going off to Dublin.

The following night I saw the pair of them off to Dublin – each with his little suitcase full of arms – on one of the cattle boats. I had decided I couldn't go with them. But when I got home, having seen them off, I discovered my lovely little .32 was gone. My mother had found it in my bedroom, wrapped it up in a handkerchief, and took it to the bridge on Stanley Road where she dropped it in the canal.

My mother gave me hell.

'Ah, don't be shouting at me,' I said. 'I could have gone to Dublin with Jackson and Comerford. I didn't have to stay behind. I could have joined the Active Service Unit.'

'Aren't you still serving your apprenticeship?' she said. 'Didn't we work hard to put you through the Technical School? After everything we've done for you! ...'

I thought that was the end of it all, but a few days later I was told to mobilise everyone for a meeting of the company to be held in the Irish National Foresters' Hall in Great Howard Street on the next Thursday night at eight o'clock, and not to forget to be there myself as there was to be a court-martial.

I wondered what it could be all about. I thought Joe Jackson was right after all: that the company was mad because we'd done something and they were just sitting on their backsides.

There were about eighteen Volunteers at the meeting which was held in a bare front room, and we sat on the benches while Tom Kerr stood at a little table up in front. Sitting beside him at the table was Stephen Lanigan who rarely came to our meetings. Steve was a senior official with the Customs and Excise Branch in Liverpool, and lived on Stanley Road opposite the North Park. He was in the IRB, and because he was so deeply involved in the smuggling of guns and ammunition, he was careful to stay away as much as possible from demonstrations, ceilis, and meetings of the Volunteers.

Tom called me to stand up.

'You made a raid for arms?' he asked.

'Of course I did!' I said, very cheekily.

'Why?' asked Tom.

'For Ireland!' I replied, bold as brass.

Everyone looked at each other, and there was a lot of subdued talk among the Volunteers. Tom Kerr and Steve Lanigan sat together and had a private conversation with each other for a few moments, and then Tom called me to attention.

'You did a very wrong thing, Seán,' he said. 'I want to explain something to you, and all the rest of you. We have special channels from England to Ireland; we've had them for years and they've never been discovered. When you make a raid like that on your own, without us knowing anything about it, our dumps and routes could be discovered. The police will make a sweep through Liverpool like the one they made in 1917: they'll raid Irish homes all over the city and they might stumble on one of our arms dumps. Then we're finished. One dump leads to another.'

'I didn't realise that,' I said, feeling very ashamed.

'In future,' warned Tom, 'no Volunteer touches guns or ammunition unless we give him permission. We'll handle that.'

When someone said that Jackson and Comerford should be court-martialled, someone else said they'd fought in 1916 and were Volunteers in the Dublin Brigade. Then someone else said that Joe Jackson might have fought in 1916 but wasn't in any Dublin company of the Volunteers. And someone else said that Joe Comerford wasn't in the Volunteers either, and that he'd never had anything to do with the Volunteers. I learned later that Jackson and Comerford were the pride and joy of the Dublin Brigade when they arrived in Dublin with the haul of revolvers and ammunition we took from the shop in Dale Street. At that time revolvers were worth their weight in gold in Dublin, and Jackson and Comerford sold them to the lads in the

Dublin Brigade. They were two of the slickest jackeens that ever left Dublin. But they did manage to get arms desperately needed by the Volunteers in Dublin.

One of the dumps used by Jackson and Comerford was a house owned by a Dublin couple, the Mahers, at Miller's Bridge near the Liverpool docks. The Mahers had a young lad called Tommy. One day Tommy found a revolver under a cushion and took it out to the back yard to shoot a cat, but he accidentally shot himself. His parents rushed him off to the Bootle General Hospital and when the Liverpool police wanted to know where he got the gun, the boy told them what his parents had told him to say: that he'd found it in the back alley.

I met Tommy Maher a few years later when I came out of the National Army and started a book with Jack Hagan, and hired Tommy as one of my runners to cover the Baggot Street area. Then I ran into him a few years ago when I was helping to organise a meeting of the Liverpool Old IRA, here in Dublin. Tommy came along and asked to join. I knew he hadn't been a Volunteer, but didn't want to say a word or embarrass him. One of the others asked him if he had a pension which would have been proof of his service.

'Oh, yes,' he said. 'I have a disability pension. I was shot.'

When Tommy died a couple of years ago, I went to his funeral. Then I read his obituary in the paper – the usual *Irish Press* stuff – which said he'd 'served in the 3rd Liverpool Battalion, IRA during the War of Independence ... his home at Miller's Bridge, Bootle, was used as a base by the IRA and during engagements in the Liverpool area he was wounded and confined to hospital under guard for some time ...'

When the Irish Civil War broke out, Joe Jackson became a detective at Oriel House, the Dublin headquarters of the Free State detectives. He was one of their best men, tough and merciless. Joe survived the Civil War to later become a bodyguard-chauffeur for Joe McGrath. He had, in fact, been a member of the Boland's Mill Garrison in the 1916 Rising, and when he died, President de Valera attended the removal of his remains.

Joe's brother Frank, who had sailed out of Liverpool as a ship's cook, went with the anti-Treatyites. One day in Dublin Frank was walking down Dame Street towards the corner of Great George's Street when a Crossley tender came tearing along with a full load of National Army troops. Frank reached into his pocket and hurled a grenade at the tender, but the boys in the tender saw him and riddled him the moment he let go with the grenade.

The police sweep of the Irish homes and boarding houses throughout Liverpool in 1917 (to which Tom Kerr referred during my court-martial) resulted from an unauthorised raid for arms made by a group of Volunteers from Dublin. The party was led by Frank Gascoigne and included Seán Hayes, Joe Jackson, Hughie and Jack Early, Ryan, Murphy, Green, and a fellow from Cork with a name like Haney. Pat Lawson, who was a member of both the IRB and the Active Service Unit, was second-in-command to Frank Gascoigne and in later years confirmed the story to me. On arriving in Liverpool the party split up and Pat found lodgings with a family named Cavanagh who lived in Commercial Road, Sandhills.

The first of the two raids plannned by the group was to be made on the Territorial Hall in Everton Valley on the same night that a big ceilí dance was to be held in Liverpool. The Dublin volunteers were to attend the dance where they were to meet a number of Cumann na mBan girls who would assist them in the raid.

The raid took place after the dance and the Volunteers got away with seventeen rifles and a large quantity of ammunition. Pat and another Volunteer teamed up with Kathleen and Sheila Brown and carried two rifles each to the Browns' home at No. 4 Laburnam Grove, Litherland. Romance had evidently got the better part of Volunteers Murphy and Ryan who, instead of taking part in the raid, had gone off with Misses Mason and McNance respectively.

The following morning, the police and Special Branch detectives began a search for the missing rifles and made enquiries at a number of Irish boarding houses throughout the city. One of the houses they visited was where Hughie Early and Green were staying, but since the two lads were out at the time, the detectives left word that they'd like to see the pair and would call back later. When Early and Green returned to their lodgings and learned that the detectives wanted to meet them, they tore down to the Pier Head without telling any of the other Volunteers and caught the boat to Dublin.

The next day there was consternation and disappointment among the remainder of the group when they discovered that the two Volunteers had fled to Dublin. Knowing that the police would then soon be on their trail, they abandoned their plan for the second arms raid and left Liverpool that night for Dublin.

3

IRELAND'S WAR OF INDEPENDENCE ENTERED its fiercest and most crucial stage with the activities of the Black and Tans[10] which began in April, 1920. Unable to crush the IRA whose tactics of guerrilla warfare proved to be so successful, the British forces of occupation in Ireland turned increasingly to such savagery that the period after July, 1920 is best described as the Reign of Terror.[11]

The Black and Tans had stepped up their terror campaign in Ireland so sharply during the summer of 1920 that many young Irishmen were leaving their homes and crossing to Liverpool, where they lodged near the docks until they could get a ship to America. So many single young men were fleeing from Ireland that IRA Headquarters became alarmed at the sudden exodus and ordered a halt to the emigration, declaring it the duty of such men to remain in Ireland and fight the enemy. It was widely rumoured – even at IRA Headquarters – that many of the emigrants were informers and renegades, and the Liverpool company of the Volunteers was instructed to raid some of the boarding houses in the dock area and seize the passports of those who had recently arrived from Ireland.

Accordingly, at a meeting of the company one evening in the Foresters' Hall in Great Howard Street, we split up into three groups of eight Volunteers each and set out to raid some of the Irish boarding houses in Nelson Street and along the dock road.

In my party the Number-one man – the tallest Volunteer looking most like a detective – knocked at the front door of the first boarding house we came to while the rest of the party scattered and kept out of sight. When the door opened, the Number-one man announced that he was a Special Branch policeman and stepped inside. As soon as he did so, I – the Number-two man – followed on his heels and then dashed through the hallway to the back door and drew my revolver to prevent anyone escaping. While some of the party remained outside and covered the front of the house, the rest came in to search the place and round up the lodgers.

While the house was being searched there was a knock on the back door and for a moment I thought it was the police, but when I opened the door I found it was only one of the lodgers returning for his supper and let him in. But as soon as he was inside and saw my revolver, he turned and dashed out again, trying to escape through the back yard, and I tore after him threatening to shoot him if he did not stop and come back. Fortunately for both of us, the poor fellow stopped and returned to join the rest of the lodgers who, by that time, had been rounded up and herded into the kitchen.

The lodgers were a badly frightened lot, especially when we seized their passports, but we told them to calm down and try to relax, as we weren't going to hurt them. Then we lectured them about their running away from Ireland, telling them that they should have stayed with their countrymen who were fighting the Black and Tans.

They told us that they hated the British government in Ireland and fully supported the Sinn Féin movement and the Volunteers, but that they'd been forced to flee from Ireland. One of them told us that he'd left Ireland after the Black and Tans shot his brother and threatened to shoot him, too, unless he got out of the country. A young woman told us that she'd left Ireland because the Tans had burnt her house to the ground.

As each lodger told us why he or she had left Ireland, we saw that they were just ordinary young Irish men and women whom the Black and Tans had forced to flee from their homes and their country. We began to realise that the story of them being traitors and renegades was a cruel lie. We felt very sorry for them and handed back their passports. We warned the boarding-house keeper to keep his mouth shut about our visit and not to go near the police, and then we split up and quietly left the house in pairs.

As I made my way home with Mick Horan, I couldn't help thinking that what we'd said to the young men and women in the boarding house applied to some of the Volunteers in our company. Several of them had arrived in Liverpool since 1916 and had no family or other ties to keep them there. *They* should have been back in

Ireland where the fighting and dying was taking place.

Shortly after the boarding house raids, the company got bolder and began training exercises and outdoor manoeuvres on the Aintree Racecourse where the Grand National Steeplechase was run every year. Few of the thousands of people who've seen the Grand National have ever imagined that the Liverpool Company of the Irish Republican Army used to do extended order drills on those fields! But I eventually became impatient with the drills and asked our O/C, Tom Kerr, for permission to go to Dublin to join the ASU, but Tom refused, saying that my place was in Liverpool where I was more valuable to the Volunteers, and besides, we would soon be preparing for a special job.

IRA Headquarters had become increasingly alarmed at the amount of wanton destruction in Ireland caused by the Black and Tans, and voices in Dublin were demanding that reprisals be carried out in England. Loudest of those voices was that of Cathal Brugha[12] who went so far as to suggest that Volunteers of the IRA should machine-gun members of parliament in the House of Commons. Michael Collins had difficulty in restraining Brugha from his most extreme proposals, but eventually IRA Headquarters ordered reprisals to be carried out in England in retaliation for what was happening in Ireland.

On the night of 20 September 1920, the Black and Tans had driven from their headquarters at Gormanston Camp and carried out the infamous 'Sack of Balbriggan.' On 1 November 1920 – the same day that Terence MacSwiney was buried in Cork[13] – Kevin Barry was hanged by the British in Mountjoy Prison. Three weeks later, on 21 November ('Bloody Sunday'), a detachment of Black and Tans set up a machine gun in Croke Park and fired indiscriminately into the crowd of football spectators killing twelve people and wounding sixty others. In the following week Ballykinlar Camp became an internment centre to accommodate the increasing number of Irishmen being arrested by the British.

The ordinary English people couldn't have cared less about what was happening in Ireland, being unconcerned about the reports of murder and destruction there. IRA Headquarters in Dublin wanted to impress upon the English people that a war of terror was being waged in their name against the Irish people, and reluctantly ordered massive reprisals to be carried out in England to show the English the sort of havoc that was being wrought in Ireland.

At a meeting of our company one evening in late September or early October 1920 at No. 93 Scotland Road, we were given the broad outline of a plan for a devastating reprisal to be carried out in Liverpool. As we listened to the plan being described, we were overawed both by its originality and by its potential for destruction. We were going to wreck the second largest dock system in the British empire.

Almost all the major docks on the Liverpool side of the River Mersey had a pair of huge dock gates and a pumping station at their entrances. The gates were opened at high tide to allow ships to enter and were then closed behind the ships to prevent the water in the docks from running out with the ebb tide. Tom Kerr's plan was for us to blow up several of the dock gates and pumping stations at low tide so that the waters inside the docks would rush out and the ships would keel over. Tom had also planned to destroy the storage tanks at Dingle Point so that the ebb tide would carry thousands of gallons of burning oil down the Mersey. If our plan succeeded, the port of Liverpool would be paralysed and the cost of the damage would be astronomical.

Two of us – Mick Horan, a brass finisher, and I – were detailed to blow up the gates and the pumping station at the Langton dry docks which were close enough to Marsdens (where I was serving my apprenticeship) that I could visit the docks without arousing anyone's suspicion.

When I ambled in to the pumping station and the fellow in charge asked me what I wanted, I told him that I was an apprenticed fitter and wanted to see for myself how the dock pumps worked. He was delighted to show me around and described the operation of the pumping station so well that I soon learned the location of the station's vital parts – and where charges of dynamite could do the most damage!

When the plan for destroying the Liverpool docks was complete, Jack Plunkett[14] came over from IRA Headquarters in Dublin to inspect the plan and then returned to Dublin with a report on the plan's feasibility.

No date had been set for the destruction of the docks, but on the night of 10 November 1920, about four weeks after the plans had been drawn up, a British army captain discovered Plunkett's report in Dublin during a raid on the home of Professor Hayes.[15] Dick Mulcahy, who was then Chief of Staff of the IRA, had been studying the report in the home of Professor Hayes at the time of the raid and narrowly avoided capture by escaping through a skylight in the roof.

IRA Headquarters quickly sent us word that our plans had been discovered, and we had to abandon the operation. The British newspapers then published an account of the discovery of the plans and the authorities immediately tightened security around the dock gates and the pumping stations. As disappointed as we were with the news that the British had stumbled across Jack Plunkett's report, it was some consolation for us to learn that his report hadn't included any mention of a diversionary tactic which had been planned to take place in conjunction with the blowing up of the Liverpool dock gates and pumping stations.

In order to distract the police and cause as much confusion as possible within the vicinity of the docks prior to our setting the charges of dynamite at the dock gates, we planned to start a number of fires in some of the warehouses and timber yards adjacent to the docks. Since we were no longer able to achieve what had been our main objective, the officers of our company then decided that we make the burning of the warehouses and timber yards a major operation.

One evening during a parade at No. 93 Scotland Road, Tom Kerr – with Steve Lanigan beside him – addressed us. Our number had risen to about thirty Volunteers by this time. Some subsequent accounts have claimed that more than twice that number of men belonged to the Liverpool Company, but I clearly remember that at that meeting we were drawn up in two lines of about fifteen men each. Tom told us that there was a special job coming up and that we'd be taking grave risks. He warned us that it was almost certain there'd be shooting, and that if we were caught, anything could happen, so that no man should come into this job unless he was fully satisfied that what he was doing was right. He appealed especially for anyone who felt he wasn't able to take the risks involved to step forward, and to be assured that no word would ever be said to him as long as he lived: that he would rather have the man step out then than fail us during the job.

Two men stepped out. After the two of them left, Tom and Steve turned to Phil Coyne, a man much older than the rest of us. Phil was a slenderly built, middle-aged man with greying hair. Tom and Steve told him that he couldn't go with us on this particular job, because it was too risky for him, a married man with a family of children. We all admired Phil; we knew he had great spirit – he would have stuck with us through thick and thin – but Tom and Steve couldn't let him take the risks.

We were divided into small groups and each of us was given his job. I suggested to Tom that the thousands of barrels of resin stored at the Shore Road, near the entrance to the Gladstone Dock, was an ideal target; once lit, they would burn like a huge torch, and would be almost impossible to extinguish and would burn down everything along the dock. But Tom disallowed this, and instead, told four of us – Bernie Meehan, Seán Harrington, a fellow called Murphy, and myself – to set fire to the timber yards that extended from the bottom of Grove Street to Regent Road or the dock road, as we called it.

None of us – Tom Kerr, his father Neill, nor Steve Lanigan – knew it at the time, but it had been planned that IRA Volunteers in the Liverpool, London, and Glasgow Companies would set fires to the warehouses and timber yards of their respective cities on the same night. Unfortunately, as the date set for the simultaneous operations grew nearer, it was realised at IRA Headquarters that only the Liverpool Company was ready to carry out its plan. Rory O'Connor, who was Director of Engineering and O/C Great Britain, came over from Dublin on Friday night, 26 November, to tell the Kerrs and

Steve Lanigan that the London and Glasgow Companies weren't ready and the Liverpool Company could cancel its plan. But the Kerrs and Steve Lanigan were for proceeding with their plan regardless of the London and Glasgow Companies, and finally, at 3.00am on Saturday morning, Rory O'Connor agreed that we should carry out our plan.

About half-past seven in the evening of Saturday, 27 November Bernie Meehan, Seán Harrington, Murphy, and myself met at the top of Grove Street and marched down to the timber yards. Later on, I thought how stupid this was – four men marching together on their way to burn down a timber yard! While Bernie and Seán got over the wall into the yard, I remained on the lookout, because if it were necessary to speak to a passer-by, my Liverpool accent would not arouse the suspicions that an Irish brogue would; furthermore, if there were trouble, my presence on Grove Street could be more easily explained than my mates', because I lived near there. Then Murphy staggered up to me and I realised he was rotten drunk. Murphy was almost middle-aged and loved his beer, but he had a coal yard in Island Road – just off Marsh Lane – and was valuable to the company because he could store arms and munitions in his coal bags and carry them around in his cart to other arms dumps pretending he was delivering coal.

A couple of people out for the evening – it was a very nice evening – came walking along Grove Street and I was afraid Murphy would be sick and attract their attention, but they passed by quietly. Then Murphy said he was feeling sick and had to go home; he pulled a revolver out of his pocket, gave it to me and told me to shoot anyone who tried to stop us.

When we got our job done, the three of us walked back together, up Grove Street and Cranworth Street to Rimrose Road. By the time we reached Rimrose Road, the timber yard was blazing away and we were hoping and praying no one was noticing us.

Bernie left us at Rimrose Road to return to my home in Wordsworth Street where he was staying. Seán Harrington lived in Litherland, and I walked with him through Hemer Terrace, as far as Bibby's

Lane. I told Seán I had Murphy's revolver, and Seán told me to hand it over to him, that he had orders to collect all revolvers. I gave it to him but promised to report it to Tom Kerr.

After he left, I noticed a fire alarm box on the corner of Bibby's Lane. I'd always wanted to ring a fire alarm, and here was my big chance: I just walked up to it, smashed the glass, and pulled the alarm. By this time the fire was burning so well, the blaze could be seen for miles, and people living in Bibby's Lane and Rimrose Road were beginning to pour into the streets.

A big, red-faced bobby soon came puffing along. 'Eh,' I said to him in my best – or worst! – Liverpool accent, 'wot the 'ell's goin' on?'

'Bleedin' fire!' he muttered. 'Those bleedin' Sinn Féiners.'

'Shinners?' I said. 'Bolshies, more like it! ... effin' Russians, I'd say.'

'Bankhall, too!' he said, looking towards the city and pointing out the clouds of smoke climbing upwards.

I left him there, confused and bewildered by it all, and made my way home. Bernie Meehan was there already, and the two of us went upstairs to watch the flames from the timber yard getting higher and higher, and the smoke clouds rising in columns from various points near the docks told us the other lads had done their jobs.

My mother came up and got suspicious, and without saying a word to either of us, started saying her prayers. Soon she and the rest of the family were gathered in the kitchen, praying.

Bernie and I could hardly wait to get the Sunday morning papers and see how much damage had been done. The papers said that all the timber yards and warehouses along the docks – eight miles of them – from Seaforth to Garston had been burned down. 'Raging infernos,' one newspaper described the fires. 'Warehouses ten storeys high were gutted to the ground.' Another paper said that over £1,000,000 worth of damage had been done, and we knew that was a modest estimate. By Monday morning it was revealed that at one time on Saturday night at least fifteen separate fires were burning, and the estimate of damage had gone up to several million pounds worth. *The Times*[16] reported that there were about 800,000 bales of cotton stored in Liverpool warehouses, and the value of a bale of cotton ranged from £25 to £35, depending upon the quality. The damage done at the Effington Street warehouse alone was in the region of £400,000. Altogether, fourteen warehouses and four timber yards had been completely destroyed. The fire brigades from Liverpool and Bootle were kept so busy they had to be reinforced by brigades from Waterloo and Crosby, even from as far away as Birkenhead, Warrington, and St Helens! The prosecution said at Neill Kerr's trial later on that twenty-three separate fires had been started within thirty-five minutes. Liverpool had never seen anything like it: never before in its history had so much damage been done in a single night. It wasn't until the May blitz of 1941 when German bombers dropped thousands of incendiaries that so much damage to Liverpool was again done in one night! We got a laugh reading the various estimates of the numbers of men involved in starting the fires. *The Times*[17] said at least fifty were involved.

But the night's work wasn't without its tragedy. An eighteen-year-old dock labourer, William Joseph Ward, from Upper Harrington Street had been accidentally shot and killed near a warehouse in Jordan Street.

Later that night police and detectives began a wholesale sweep through Liverpool that lasted for more than ten days, and scores of Irishmen from all parts of the city were taken into custody. Many of these were sympathetic to the Irish nationalist movement, but had nothing to do with the Volunteers and had no connection whatsoever with the warehouse and timber yard fires. Although they lacked enough evidence to convict them, the British authorities interned them anyway. In later years some of the fellows who were interned managed to collect medals and pensions from the Irish government!

To help the Liverpool police, constables and detectives were brought in from different parts of the country, and raids were made on every known meeting place for Irish nationalists. Sinn Féin Clubs, Foresters' Halls, and the local headquarters for the Irish Self-Determination League were all raided. Even Irish pubs were raided! And in one of them on Scotland Road, a Francis McPartlin was picked up on Monday, 29 November and charged with the murder of William Ward. McPartlin was, of course, completely innocent of the poor lad's death: he had nothing to do with the fires – as far as I know, he wasn't even near a warehouse on the night of the fires. But the police were desperate and blundering, and McPartlin fitted the description of the man they were looking for.

It was tragically unfortunate that Ward happened to be in Jordan Street at the time of the fires on that Saturday night. The three cotton warehouses in the neighbourhood of Jordan and Sparling Streets were set on fire about half-past eight. When Ward noticed three men acting suspiciously in a warehouse doorway, he ran off to tell a policeman – a Constable Tilley – about them. The policeman and the youth chased after the three suspects until one of the suspects stopped and turned around in Parliament Street, drew out a revolver and fired at the policeman. The bullet missed the policeman, but struck and killed young Ward.

The constable followed one of the three men into Jordan Street, where the man turned and hit the constable with a pair of bolt cutters, and then raced on. But Tilley finally caught up with the man – who'd been stopped by some civilians further along the street – and arrested him.

The man Constable Tilley arrested was Mattie Fowler – a Dubliner in our company who was living in Birkenhead – and he was jointly charged with Ward's murder. The two fellows who'd been with Mattie managed to get away, but the police had a rough description of them, and when they picked up McPartlin in the pub, they thought they had the man who'd fired the revolver.

There was another shooting incident – at Bankhall – and a second Volunteer, Jim McCaughey, was arrested and charged with attempting to murder a policeman named Sloane.

Two plainclothes policemen – Sloane and Grounds – had been standing at the corner of Sandhills Lane and Bankhall Lane when they saw a small party of men trying the several doors of the cotton warehouse in Bankhall Lane, a cul-de-sac. The two policemen went across to a doorway where a man (eighteen-year-old Tommy Moran) was busy with a pair of bolt cutters, and struggled with him as they tried to arrest him. Then someone who saw the struggle crossed over from the other side of the lane with a revolver in his hand, and forced the two policemen to release young Tommy.

A short time later, the same two policemen saw another suspect coming out of a warehouse doorway where only moments before they'd discovered four tins of paraffin. When they tried to arrest the man, he pulled out a revolver and fired at Sloane, but the bullet only tore through the sleeve of Sloane's coat. But the shot – even though it missed its mark – badly frightened the two policemen who ran away, letting the Volunteers escape scot-free.

It was after the shooting incidents that the police started looking for the ringleaders of the night's operation, and it was almost inevitable that old Neill Kerr's house in Florida Street should be raided. Neill was a well-known Sinn Féiner and one of the leading lights among the Irish nationalists in Liverpool. He had been involved in the nationalist movement for years. When O'Donovan Rossa's[18] body was brought back from America to Ireland, it was Neill Kerr who organised the pallbearers that carried Rossa's remains from one ship to the other, in accordance with Rossa's wish that his remains never touch English soil. The police probably suspected him of helping to organise the two huge Sinn Féin processions[19] when about ten thousand people marched in Bootle, Liverpool on Sunday 21 November. What they never suspected was that he was one of Mick Collins' most trusted agents: Neill's part in the arms and ammunition smuggling had been a closely kept secret.

When they raided his home later on that Saturday night, the police found – in the back room of the house – a number of documents which included a signal manual with a cipher code, a book on military engineering, a printed circular on the manufacture of firearms, and some Irish Republican Bonds. One of the detectives (David Thompson, Liverpool CID) searched Neill and found two receipts for fifteen pairs of bolt cutters worth £15 which had been bought at a tool shop in Renshaw Street, Liverpool. The detectives also found on Neill a bill made out to a John Daly on 16 November 1920, for £4's worth of repairs to a motor car.

Poor Neill! He was never able to live it down that he allowed those receipts for the bolt cutters to be found in his pockets. He was scorned and ridiculed by people not fit to blacken his shoes. What few people knew was that while he was being searched, Neill was able to keep hidden on his person the bank notes for huge sums of money to pay for arms and ammunition being smuggled to Michael Collins.

In one of the rooms of Kerr's house the detectives came across Jim McCaughey who had been sleeping there and who was wearing the uniform of an officer in the Irish Republican Army. They arrested Jim and charged him with attempting to murder Police-Constable Sloane! But once again the police had got the wrong man: the man who had fired the shot through Sloane's coat was none other than Mike O'Leary! Mike had got home all right after the shooting incident at Bankhall, and after mass on Sunday morning had taken the train to Manchester.

The police originally charged Neill Kerr with conspiring with Jim McCaughey to murder police officers 'and other persons,' and they also charged them with conspiring to set fire to warehouses. But neither Neill nor Jim had been anywhere near the fires – they had been to a ceilí held in St Joseph's Hall! The uniform Jim was wearing when arrested belonged to one of Neill's sons, and Jim wore it to the ceilí to show people who'd never seen what a Volunteer officer's uniform looked like.

The search for the 'conspirators' reached as far as Scotland where a Volunteer named Harry Coyle was arrested, brought to Liverpool and charged with conspiracy in connection with the warehouse fires. Harry Coyle was the 'John Daly' to whom the receipt for motor-car repairs found on Neill Kerr referred.

Harry Coyle from Co. Mayo was a brigade-adjutant in the IRA. His job was to run guns and munitions (which the Glasgow Volunteers had collected) from Glasgow to Liverpool, where they were 'dumped' until they could be smuggled across to Ireland. He had been in Liverpool on 16 November – the date of the receipt found on Kerr – getting repairs to a five-seater motor-car which belonged to a fellow named McCabe who lived in Glasgow. Harry was in Glasgow on 29 November, and when he was passing through Dunfermline at midnight on 4 December, two Dunfermline policemen noticed that he had no lights and tried to stop him, but he drove on. In trying to stop him, the policemen had got close enough to his car to see two rifles, and they chased after him in their car until they caught up with him. When they did, the police found that Harry was driving a mobile arsenal – the car contained three hundred pounds of gelignite, detonators, fuses, rifles, ammunition, and three fully-loaded automatic pistols.

In trying to link Harry Coyle with the fires, the police were wide of the mark once more: Coyle had nothing to do with the fires – he had the much more important job of running guns and munitions!

The discovery by the police of a unique paraffin container at the site of one of the fires led to the arrest on 5 December of the only two women charged in connection with the fires. When the container was found, the police published its description in the Liverpool papers and asked any chandler or oil merchant who recognised the container or remembered its owner to come forward. Sure enough, someone recognised the unusual container and remembered the customers – Kathleen and Sheila Brown. Kathleen and Sheila were sisters – two lovely girls – who lived in Laburnum Grove, Litherland. They were both active in the Cumann na mBan and attended the ceilís at the Roger Casement Sinn Féin Club in Bridge Road. Sheila was a schoolteacher, and Kathleen worked as a clerk at John Hughes' in Liverpool where my sister Mary was one of the chief cashiers.

The Browns' house was raided on Tuesday evening, 30 November. A detective (Det. Inspector Peter Gregson of the Lancashire County Police) found a stack of Sinn Féin literature which included copies of the Proclamation of the Irish Republic, Sinn Féin membership cards, subscription lists, and most important of all, a letter addressed to 'Florie or JOC' which dealt with the purchase of ammunition, detonators, spare machine-gun bolts, and cartridge cases – and signed 'SH'. There was also a balance sheet found which recorded purchase of revolvers and travelling expenses to Liverpool. A few days later, on 5 December, the house was searched again, and a detective (Det. Sergeant Leabourne of Seaforth Police Station) came across three old oil cans which had been burnt and damaged. As a result of these discoveries, the Brown girls were charged with conspiracy to murder, and conspiracy to set fire to storehouses and warehouses.

The eighth and final person arrested and charged in connection with the fires was a Michael Brennan who was picked up some time after the fires and identified by two constables who'd been on duty in Chisenhall Street at half-past eight on the night of the fires. While chasing a man they had noticed on the street corner, the two constables had come across a gallon can of paraffin wrapped up in a paper lying in a warehouse doorway. Having examined the tin of paraffin, they looked up for their suspect, but by that time he'd disappeared: all they could hear were his footsteps fading away!

But Brennan wasn't the man they were looking for; he wasn't one of our Volunteers – as far as I know he had nothing to do with the nationalist movement! He was an innocent man mistakenly identified by a couple of stupid constables desperate for an arrest.

As a result of the enormous damage we had done, the eight people who were arrested and charged were brought before the Liverpool Police Court in Dale Street early in December 1920 where their cases gained national – and even international – publicity. Kathleen and Sheila Brown, Neill Kerr, Harry Coyle, Mattie Fowler, Jim McCaughey, Michael Brennan and Francis McPartlin were arraigned before the Stipendiary Magistrate (Stuart Deacon), with F. J. Sims (Deputy Assistant Prosecutor) representing the Director of Public Prosecutions, and Howard Roberts appearing for the crown. The main charge against the eight was 'that they conspired, with others unknown; to unlawfully and maliciously set fire to storehouses, warehouses, and buildings in the city, contrary to the provisions of the Malicious Damages Act.' Mattie Fowler and Francis McPartlin were further charged with the wilful murder of William Ward, and Jim McCaughey was charged with attempting to murder PC Sloane.

Mattie, who'd been arrested on the night of the fires, had been brought before the stipendiary magistrate on Monday 29 November, but despite the terrible beating he'd received at the hands of the

Liverpool police – he appeared in court with two black eyes and his head swathed in bandages – he refused to reveal his identity, and it wasn't until Wednesday 1 December that the authorities learned his name. On the morning of Mattie's first appearance in Liverpool Police Court, the British government was so alarmed at the previous weekend's events in Liverpool that the public galleries of the House of Commons were closed and the public wasn't even admitted to the outer lobby of the house. Those of us who knew Mattie thought the precautions very amusing!.

Mattie Fowler, Jim McCaughey, and Neill Kerr were defended by a Henry Maden,[20] while Kathleen and Sheila Brown, Harry Coyle and Michael Brennan were represented by a brilliant young Catholic lawyer named George Lynskey.[21]

The case was widely reported by the British newspapers, some of whom gave it sensational coverage. One newspaper – I believe it was the *Daily Sketch* – carried the story under the headline: 'Kathleen of the Bronze Locks and Fair Sheila Smile at Recital of Sinn Féin Plot.' The same newspaper went on to report the proceedings in the Liverpool Police Court in a style which revealed not only how low were the standards of journalism in the popular British press of the day, but also how little the English understood of the Irish nationalist movement. Typical of the report were these lines:

> Like McPartlin, Coyle was of the intellectual and student type, but Brennan and McCaughey were distinctly of the labouring class.
>
> One wondered if these were actual Sinn Féiners and representative of that body, how high intellectuality was associated with it. Perhaps their appearances form no index to their temperament and culture as the crown now endeavours to make out of fair Sheila, the teacher, and bronze Kathleen, the clerk.

Of the eight, Sheila and Kathleen Brown, Neill Kerr, Harry Coyle, Mattie Fowler, and Jim McCaughey were sent to trial before Judge Sir Alfred Tobin at the Liverpool Assizes in the second week of February, 1921. The British government's interest in the trial was so great that, in an unprecedented move, the attorney general, Sir Gordon Hewart,[22] came up to Liverpool to personally direct the prosecution of the case. Mr Ashton KC represented the crown and Mr Hemmerde KC[23] (assisted by his junior, Mr Maden) led the defence.

The evidence against Harry Coyle was flimsy and on Friday 11 February he was acquitted of the charges in connection with the fires of 27 November, although he remained in detention to face a charge (laid in Scotland) of possessing explosives. The crown also announced that the charges of conspiracy to murder against Sheila and Kathleen Brown were to be dropped, and on Saturday 12 February it announced it wasn't going to proceed any further in the case against them.

Mr Hemmerde did a magnificent job attacking the methods of the prosecution as being 'grossly unfair,' 'slipshod,' and 'discreditable,' but he was unable to win acquittals for the three who remained on trial. The jury found Neill Kerr and Jim McCaughey guilty of conspiracy to murder and to setting fire to warehouses and timber yards, and the judge sentenced each of them to ten years penal servitude. Jim McGaughey was found guilty of attempted murder and got ten years penal servitude to be served concurrently with the other sentence. Mattie Fowler (who sometimes went by the name of McGinty) was found guilty of conspiracy to set fire to warehouses and timber yards and was given the maximum sentence for that offence, two years penal servitude. Poor Mattie – God rest him! – was from Oldcastle, Co. Meath. He survived the Liverpool Bridewell and Dartmoor Prison, but was later killed in the Irish Civil War.

Mr Hemmerde launched an appeal on behalf of Neill Kerr before Justices Darling, Avory, and Slater in the Court of Criminal Appeal on Tuesday 22 March 1921, contending that there hadn't been any evidence to convict Neill of conspiracy to murder and the sentence for conspiracy to commit arson had been too heavy. Justices Avory and Darling concurred in finding that there hadn't been sufficient evidence to convict him of conspiracy to murder and the sentence was quashed. Neill's two-year sentence for conspiracy to commit arson was, however, allowed to stand.

It is understandable that Mr Justice Salter dissented from the opinion of Justices Darling and Avory and that he thought that

Neill's sentence should be affirmed. Mr Salter represented the Basingstoke Division from 1906 until 1917 as a unionist MP.

4

FOR THE NEXT COUPLE OF months after the warehouse and timber yard fires, the Liverpool Company of the Volunteers had to lie quiet, very quiet! The Liverpool police and detectives were everywhere, watching like hawks. We knew that certain Irish homes and boarding houses were being kept under surveillance, and that a close watch was being kept on the activities of known sympathisers and supporters of the movement. Another difficulty for our company was that its leadership had been hard hit. Neill Kerr was held in custody awaiting trial, while his son Tom and Stephen Lanigan were in the Dublin Bridewell before being interned at Frongoch Camp in North Wales.

The arrests of Neill Kerr, Steve Lanigan, and Henry Coyle were a severe blow to Michael Collins' network, and the steady flow of badly needed arms and munitions from Liverpool was immediately affected. IRA Headquarters in Dublin was seriously concerned about the drop in arms traffic. Collins had never been enthusiastic about Cathal Brugha's ideas for Volunteer reprisals in England, and when the results of the Liverpool fires were felt in Dublin, the gap between Collins and Brugha became wider than ever. But Collins' immediate problem was to find someone he could put in charge of the arms running in Liverpool. As Tom Kerr told me some years later, what happened was this: the Secretary of the Cumann na mBan in Dublin, Leslie Price, (who later married Tom Barry, IRA leader of the Kilmichael ambush) visited the Bridewell every day, and Collins sent in word with her to find out from Tom who should be put in charge of the arms running. Stephen Lanigan was sharing Tom's cell at the time, so the two of them discussed the problem and recommended young Paddy Daly. When Mick Collins sent word across to Liverpool that Paddy Daly was to be put in charge of the dumps and the gun-running, the older IRB men in Liverpool were wild at the idea of this young pup taking over.

Paddy Daly had been a medical student in Dublin, but because of his activities in the IRA he had to go 'on the run' and he came over to Liverpool where he got a job in a cotton warehouse on the docks. I used to meet Paddy at the ceilís in Bridge Road, and remember talking to him one evening about the Liverpool Volunteers and telling him he should join. He even came around a few times to our house in Rimrose Road, but he never let on that he already was a Volunteer and a member of the IRB! He was a highly trusted man and became one of Collins' most valuable agents. When the 'split' came and the Civil War broke out in Ireland, Paddy went with the anti-Treatyites, and when the fighting ceased he got special permission from the archbishop to complete his medical studies at Trinity College and finally became a doctor. He later joined the Irish Army Medical Corps and rose to be senior physician of St Brechin's Military Hospital. I sometimes meet him on the street now, but he doesn't recognise me anymore. Perhaps he has forgotten me, or maybe he remembers that I was in the army too – fighting for the Irish Free State.

After the warehouse fires the company had to elect a new O/C because Tom Kerr was interned. We made the biggest mistake in the company's history when we elected Hughie Early who, with his brother Jack, had come from Dublin to find work in Liverpool. I've cursed the man ever since. Because of his inexperience, several young Volunteers were captured and sentenced to long terms of penal servitude in English prisons. Their careers wrecked, some of those Volunteers ended their days in dreadful poverty.

At a parade of the company one evening in February 1921, Hughie Early lined us up and told us we were soon going to do a job. As a reprisal for the farms being destroyed by the Black and Tans all over Ireland, we were going to destroy a number of farms around Liverpool; we'd surround Liverpool with a circle of fires. He told us to team up in two's and three's and find our own farms and to be ready to destroy them when he gave the word.

I paired up with Charlie O'Gorman. Charlie and I found an ideal farm on the outskirts of Litherland. About a mile along the canal towpath from Litherland, there was a swing bridge, and on the other side of the swing bridge, a lane – like an Irish bohereen – ran for about a hundred yards and ended in a lovely big farm with several huge barns filled with hay and straw. It was an ideal target and we were delighted because we knew that after setting it on fire, our getaway would be so easy: all we would have to do would be to run back through the lane to the canal – the hedges would keep us hidden from view. When we reached the canal we would cross over the swing bridge, throw it open behind us, tear along the towpath, and then take to the back alleys in Litherland. Within seven or eight minutes of starting the fire, we could be sitting on the front steps of the Litherland Police Station as innocent as a pair of lost kittens! We knew every street and back alley in Litherland; we'd known them for years!

We were terribly disappointed when, at the next meeting, Hughie Early told eight of us – Charlie O'Gorman, Bernie Meehan, Joseph Hayes, Niall Lively, Seamus O'Malley, Tommy McGennity, Seamus Monaghan, and myself – to meet on Wednesday March 9 at Mick Horan's house in Seaforth at half-past six in the evening. He gave us no idea of what we were going to do: he just told us to be there. Although we were disappointed that we were not going to be allowed to carry out our own plan, and were not told any information about Early's plan, we thought we'd been selected for something very important, something so carefully planned that no details could be given out at that time.

The eight of us showed up all right. We sat quietly in the dark of Mick Horan's house because Hughie had said that no one was to put on the lights. In all the time we sat there, he didn't tell us a word about the job we were going to do, not a single bloody word! I was getting more uneasy all the time because I had no idea of where we were going or what we were going to do. Charlie O'Gorman whispered that he had no idea what was going on, and I soon realised that no one else seemed to know either. I sat there in the dark thinking that this was the craziest way to go about a job.

About seven o'clock, Hughie finally broke the silence and told us we were all going to go down to Seaforth station and buy train tickets to Hall Road, a little station on the electric railway line from Liverpool to Southport. He told us to carry nothing in our pockets except matches – no papers of any kind. I thought: what the hell is this? Eight Irishmen marching together down to Seaforth station and buying tickets to Hall Road! The man's mad!

All the way to Hall Road I kept wondering who could be directly responsible for this lunatic idea. I know *now* who was responsible. He's dead now. God be good to him! – and I mean it! His family were close friends of ours and his mother was very fond of me.

When the eight of us got off the train at Hall Road station it was about half-past seven and quite dark. Neither Charlie nor I had any idea of where we were going – we just followed the ones in front along a road that led into the country.

Suddenly our man up front said, 'Stop here!' Then he told us that there was a farm over on the right, and another one over on the left, but we couldn't see a damned thing in the dark. We were divided into two groups: Charlie O'Gorman, Bernie Meehan, Joseph Hayes and myself were in one group, and Seamus O'Malley, Niall Lively, Tommy McGennity and Seamus Monaghan were in the other group. Each group was to separate at that point, our group going to the farm on the left, while the other group went to the farm on the right.

Just before the two groups separated, I said, 'Wait a minute! Can anyone tell me if each farm is the same distance from this point?'

'Oh, yes!' a voice answered.

'Are you sure?' I asked. 'Because if they aren't, and one fire gets started before the other, the second group won't have a chance. They'll be spotted in the light from the first fire.'

'It's the same distance,' the voice answered, and away we went, each group heading off in a different direction. In our group, Joseph Hayes and Bernie Meehan went ahead, and Charlie and I followed, sticking close behind.

Suddenly I saw Seamus O'Malley from the other group darting across our path, ahead of us. I could see him trying to get through a wire fence, and the next thing I knew was that we were all up against a barbed wire fence! The five of us dashed along the fence trying to get through it, when all of a sudden the whole sky lit up with the flames from the fire which the other group had already started.

Quickly realising the desperate situation we were in, we dashed about frantically and were soon separated from each other. Charlie and I stuck together, but we had no idea where the others – Bernie Meehan, Joseph Hayes, and Seamus O'Malley – had gone. Jasus! The sweat broke out of us as we scurried about trying to find our way back. We had got nowhere near the farm we were supposed to set on fire, and with every second the light from the other farm was getting brighter and brighter. There was soon enough light for us to see the other two lads in our group tearing along about a hundred yards away. Seamus O'Malley had disappeared. Charlie and I ran as fast as we could and caught up with Bernie and Joseph.

The night was now quite brightly lit up from the flames of the *two* farm fires as sparks blown across the road from the first farm fire ignited hay stacks on the adjacent farm, and as the four of us ran across the open field towards the station, we knew that anyone at the station could see us. When we got to within about two hundred yards of the station, we saw the narrow footbridge that arched across the double tracks and linked the two platforms, and we knew there were spectators already on the bridge and that they'd seen us. One of the lads spotted a hollow in the ground beside a ditch and we threw ourselves into the hollow. I found Joseph Hayes lying beside me, and said to him, 'For Chris' sake, how are we going to get out of this? We can't get over the bridge. All the people up there are having a grandstand view of the fire!' Joseph didn't answer.

'How in hell are we going to get away?' I asked the others. 'Can we get cross those railway lines?'

'We can't,' someone answered. 'It's an electric line and we don't know where the electric rail is.'

'We can't stay here,' I said. 'We'll have to try and *rush* our way across the bridge. We'll fight our way!'

'We can't fight our way through all those people,' a voice said.

'Is there any other way?' I asked. 'They know damned well we're from the fires; we were lit up like flies on a wall.'

Then Joseph Hayes pulled out a revolver and said he was going to throw it away. 'Wait a minute!' I said, and grabbed it from him. 'We'll talk first! Does anyone want this revolver?'

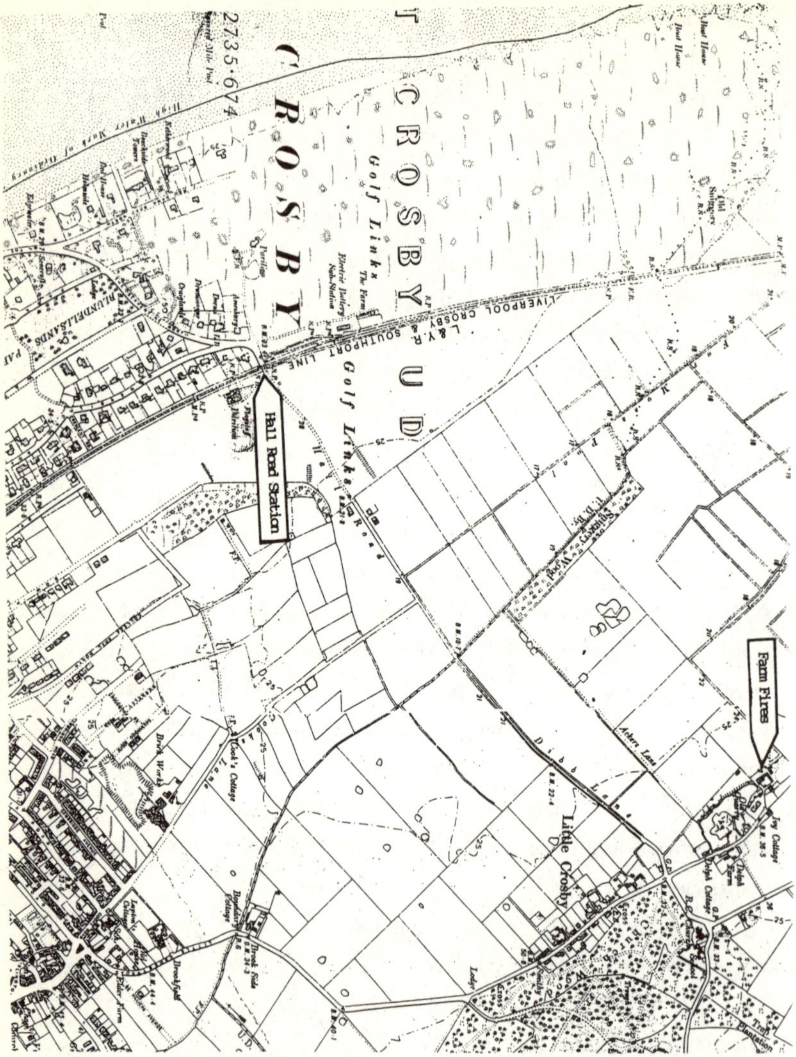

Hall Road Station and the Farm Fires (reproduced from the 1909 Ordnance Map).

No one spoke. I asked each one in turn if he wanted it. No one did.

'Right!' I said. 'If I take it and start firing ...'

'We'll be slaughtered!' said Hayes. He'd taken the words out of my mouth!

'So there's only one thing to do,' I said, and hurled the revolver into the ditch.

Since none of us knew any other way of getting across the bridge, we had to rush it. When we reached the bridge, I got in front, determined to fight my way through. I fought like a tiger – and so did the others – until I was finally pinned down by two men who nearly broke my arms as they twisted them behind my back. As they dragged me from the bridge towards the station platform, I could hear someone shouting, 'Throw him over! ... throw the bastard over!' Then I heard a train approaching and I prayed to God for the train to hurry and get into the station before they threw me onto the tracks. When we got to the platform I tried to dig my heels in, and struggled with every ounce of strength left in me to stop them from getting me to the edge of the platform. 'Throw him in!' – several people were shouting now – 'In with him! Throw the Sinn Féin bastard in!' But the train roared and shot past without even slowing down. It was an express! O Jesus, Mary and Joseph! I thanked God and began to relax. I had to: I was exhausted.

After the train disappeared in the distance, I was dragged back across the bridge and thrown with the others into a tiny little waiting-room, and the door was locked behind us. We were glad that door was locked! If it hadn't been, I'm afraid we would have been lynched!

Shortly afterwards, a big railway policeman came in. 'Boys,' he said as he shook his head slowly, 'I've got to ask you your names. The police will be here in a few minutes. I'm a railway detective.'

None of us would say a word. He was nice and mild-mannered. I wondered what sort of trickery he was up to. 'Boys,' he said once more, 'I must have your names and addresses.' He seemed sympathetic towards us as he stood there slowly shaking his head. We often wondered afterwards if he was a Liverpool-Irish Catholic because many of the railway police were Catholics. But we were under orders not to give our names, and I wouldn't dream of telling him mine. Then someone spoke and gave his name. O my God, I thought, the first one has cracked! Then another gave his name, and then another. And then I gave my name ... and suddenly felt terribly ashamed that I, too, had broken an order not to reveal our identity.

Almost immediately the station was swarming with policemen. They came into the little waiting-room and we were quickly handcuffed, thrown into a van and taken to Waterloo Police Station. We hadn't been long in the police station, before who walked in but ... me bould Seamus O'Malley!

Seamus was a railway fireman, and when he got separated from the rest of his group after the first fire got started, he headed straight for the railway line. He knew every inch of the line and it was nothing for him to cross the tracks safely. He'd got over the tracks and made his way to the sand dunes on the far side along the shore. Then he walked out to the water's edge and headed back to Liverpool. He legged it as fast as he could but ran into a line of police strung across the beach.

From Waterloo Police Station we were taken to Seaforth Police Station where we were searched and kept overnight. The next morning we were sent to Islington Police Station in Liverpool and held for identification. The identification parade was a farce. We were put in line with a bunch of tramps – old, unshaven men in ragged clothes who were picked up from the alleys of Liverpool's slums. A detective walked behind us as we were being identified. One of the people who identified us was the man from the signal box at Hall Road station – he said he'd been watching us all the time from when we'd got off the bloody train! It was he who later testified in court that each of us carried a parcel under his arm.

After the so-called identification parade at Islington Police Station, we were taken to the Liverpool Bridewell in Dale Street – but not before the police tried to scare the hell out of us. While we were waiting in our cells to be taken to the Bridewell, we could hear the police saying to each other: ' ... and what is the number of your rifle? ... got your revolver? ... did he get enough rounds of ammunition? ...'

While we were held at Dale Street Bridewell, we learned that barns of grain and hay had been set on fire at thirteen different farms surrounding Merseyside on the evening of our arrest. Three farms had been struck in Crosby; six on the outskirts of Liverpool in Woolton, Childwall, Wavertree, and West Derby; two at Wallasey; one at Bidston; and one at Aughton. Then on Thursday night, 10 March a large Dutch barn had been destroyed at Moor Farm, Little Crosby, belonging to a William Appleton whose son-in-law, Captain Reynolds, was one of the hated Auxiliary Cadets of the RUC rampaging Ireland.

The rash of farm fires continued throughout the remainder of March. On Saturday night, 12 March three bays of wheat valued at £800 were destroyed at the Model Farm, Lymm, Cheshire, and on the weekend of 19 and 20 March a total of thirty-six ricks of grain and hay were destroyed on the southern outskirts of London. During the same weekend there were also farm fires on the outskirts of Manchester.

We vowed that if we got the chance to do so, we'd escape from the Bridewell in order to punish Hughie Early for the fiasco which led to our arrest. Bernie Meehan and Seamus O'Malley were determined that Early should be shot.

At the Dale Street Bridewell we were joined by a sixth Volunteer, Paddy Lowe, who'd been captured while attempting to set fire to a farm at Huyton on the south-eastern outskirts of Liverpool. Paddy Lowe and Volunteer Jim NcNance were entering the Roby Farm at a quarter to eight on the evening of Wednesday 9 March when Mr Rimmer, the owner of the farm, and one of Rimmer's labourers surprised the two Volunteers. Rimmer fired his shotgun at Paddy Lowe hitting him in the leg, and Jim McNance promptly fled the scene leaving poor Paddy hanging onto a wire fence where the police caught and arrested him. To the best of my knowledge Paddy Lowe was the only Volunteer of the Liverpool Company to have been wounded in the course of all our activities.

The White Cross[24] was very good to us while we were kept at the Bridewell. They arranged for two lawyers – Lynskey (who'd done such an excellent job defending the fellows arrested after the warehouse fires) and Maden – to defend us in court. The White Cross also arranged with the Bridewell's caterers to send us three full meals a day, but by the time we got the food, the bloody guards had taken half of it – they even took half the cigarettes sent in to us! It was customary at the Bridewell for the guards to help themselves to half of all the stuff brought in for the prisoners.

At the Bridewell we were interrogated by a number of detectives, one of whom was Inspector Moore of the CID. He was a big, jovial, red-faced man from Co. Leitrim!

On Thursday 31 March 1921 the six of us were brought before the magistrates at the Islington Police Court where Joseph Hayes, Seamus O'Malley, Bernie Meehan, Charlie O'Gorman and I were jointly charged with setting fire to a quantity of hay and corn stored in a barn belonging to John Rainford at White House Farm, Little Crosby, and of setting fire to a quantity of hay and corn in a barn on an adjacent farm managed by Mr Rainford for the estate of the late Elizabeth Rainford of Hill Farm, Little Crosby. The total damage done at the two farms was estimated at £3,600.

In a separate indictment, Paddy Lowe was charged with having attempted to set fire to stacks of hay and grain on the property of John Rimmer of Roby Farm, Huton, and also of possessing firearms with intent to endanger life.

The Director of Public Prosecutions was represented by S. Pearce, and George Lynskey appeared on our behalf.

Detective-Sergeant Moffat, the chief witness for the prosecution, claimed he found on Hayes a five-chambered revolver which was loaded with three cartridges, and also a life preserver made from a length of steel pipe.

He said that at the time of my arrest he noticed I spoke with an English accent and asked me if I was an Englishman.

'No,' I said. 'I'm Irish and proud of it, too.'

'An Irishman born in England?' he asked sarcastically.

'Yes,' I said, 'unfortunately!'

Someone in the courtroom laughed, and next day my reply was printed in the papers and became an expression heard for years afterwards in Liverpool: ' ... born in England? yes, unfortunately!'

Evidence was then given by a Sergeant Rawcliffe who described the capture of Seamus O'Malley on the Crosby shore, and the prosecution returned to the matter of the fires. We were disgusted, however, as police witnesses presented a mass of fabricated evidence to 'prove' that Joseph Hayes, Bernie Meehan, Charlie O'Gorman and I had started the fires. The police claimed that our footprints – including mine – led to the barns, but despite the objections of our defence counsel that the police had produced no tangible proof – such as plaster casts of our footprints – to support their claim, the court accepted the testimony of the police.

The only solid evidence the police were able to produce was a religious medal which they said they'd found hanging on a twig near White House Farm. They said that Seamus O'Malley had claimed it belonged to him and, furthermore, that Charlie O'Gorman and I wore 'somewhat similar' medals.

Joseph Hayes had no revolver on him when he was arrested on Hall Road station. The police must have subsequently found his revolver in the ditch where I'd thrown it, and had somehow managed to pin ownership of the revolver on Hayes. The only weapon Joseph Hayes possessed when he was arrested was a length of steel pipe bound with tape.

Lynskey submitted to the court that there was no case for us to answer on any of the charges, but nevertheless the magistrates remanded us to Walton Prison while we awaited trial at the Liverpool Assizes.

Paddy Lowe was still limping so badly from his gunshot wounds that he had to be assisted from the court, but the rest of us left the courtroom stunned by the realisation that we'd been ordered – on the basis of concocted evidence no stronger than a piece of string on a religious medal – to stand trial for offences we hadn't been able to commit. We wished to hell we *had* lit those fires, but the fiasco of the evening's operation near Hall Road needed only the final irony of our trial in order to be complete.

When we got to Walton Prison, we were stripped of everything we had – even my last few cigarettes were snatched by the detectives who'd brought us to the prison. We knew we were going to be in for a rough time at Walton, and I knew I was going to have a rougher time of it than the others. Word was soon passed along among the warders that I was born in England, and in their eyes this made me worse than the lads I was arrested with.

The medical examination was a joke! We were all brought into a big empty room and told to strip off; then we stood there in the nude for about half an hour until the doctor finally came in. When he did, he just glanced around at us – at our faces! You could see the hatred he had for us by the look in his eyes. When he looked at me, I just grinned back at him, and he went wild and ordered us out.

Our cells were crawling with cockroaches, and when I told the Catholic chaplain about them, he promised to speak to the prison authorities. But the prison authorities told the priest there was nothing they could do about them, because the cockroaches came in the mailbags which were brought to the prison for repairs. Those mailbags must have come from all parts of the world; you could even smell the tropical dampness on some of them. Within a couple of days we were all sick, and I wondered if it was the result of the cockroaches or because we were being given rotten food.

The Catholic chaplain, Canon St John, was very good to us. He was so kind and sympathetic. Everyone else at Walton Prison was a swine, but the canon was a living saint. Someone said that he was a convert: that he'd been an Anglican vicar but had joined the Catholic Church and became a priest. He was so good to us that when we were finally released from prison, the Liverpool Cumann na mBan presented him with a beautifully illuminated address on behalf of all the IRA prisoners who'd been in Walton.[25] The address was made by John Morgan who looked after the St James' Catholic Repository off Marsh Lane, in Bootle, and who was a Gaelic speaker. It was the most beautiful piece of Irish manuscript writing I've ever seen: all our names were on it, and six copies were made. Besides the one given to Canon St John, Mrs Lennox of the Cumann na mBan got one, John Morgan kept one, and I got one – for being the youngest prisoner, I suppose! I took my copy to Dublin with me, but it was lost from my kit bag when I was moving from one barracks to another. I broke my heart trying to find it, but I never saw it again.

The only nice thing I remember about Walton was the chapel where we heard mass. It was a beautiful little chapel and had been donated by John Hughes whose shops were all over Liverpool. John Hughes was a great Catholic and great Irishman; he had been sentenced to nine months in Walton for helping Irishmen avoid conscription during the Great War.

I'll never forget one of the prisoners I met at Walton. Instead of the usual convict's uniform he wore a dark grey suit, and he strode along the prison halls as if he were still in the army. Whenever he met us he'd always give us a big grin and say, 'Fine day for the hay!' and stride on. He was a big fellow from the west – a Connaught Ranger. The Connaught Rangers were stationed in the Punjab – no Irish regiment was allowed to stay in Ireland – and mutinied when they heard what the Black and Tans were doing in Galway. The British government tried to hush up news of the mutiny and the subsequent court-martials of sixty-nine rangers of whom fourteen were sentenced to be shot and forty-six were given sentences of penal servitude ranging from one year to twenty years. Thirteen of the fourteen rangers sentenced to death had their sentences commuted to penal servitude for life, but one poor fellow – James Daly from Tyrellspass – was executed. The Ranger we met at Walton was there by himself, because the British decided that penal servitude for life wasn't enough punishment: they had to be doubly cruel and isolate the lads from their comrades. It showed how much the mutiny must have stung the British.[26] Of course, most of the regiment's officers were 'horse Protestants' – sons of English landlords in Ireland. But Walton didn't take a feather out of that Ranger. 'Fine day for the hay! ... 'Great man!'

Our trial at the Liverpool Assizes began on Friday 8 April 1921 before Justice Rigby Swift[27] who'd been elected to parliament as a Conservative MP in December 1910, and who'd been appointed to the King's Bench division of the High Court in June 1920 on the recommendation of none other than Lord Birkenhead.[28] When the judge entered the courtroom – with all the pomp and ceremony the English legal system provides for such occasions – he looked for all the world like an admiral from *The Pirates of Penzance!* By that time neither my comrades nor I had anything but contempt for British justice, but I particularly despised the pageantry of the courtroom because it seemed to me to have been designed to overawe and intimidate the prisoner. It must have been a terrifying experience for any member of the English working class to be in the dock.

There were five counts against each of us – Seamus O'Malley, Joseph Hayes, Bernie Meehan, Charlie O'Gorman, and myself – under the headings of arson, conspiracy, and 'having possession of firearms and ammunition with intent to endanger life or to enable other persons by means thereof to endanger life, or to cause serious injury to property.'

Seamus O'Malley and Joseph Hayes were defended by Mr Maden, while Bernie Meehan, Charlie O'Gorman, and I were defended by Mr Lynskey.

The crown was represented by Alexander T. Miller, KC, an ex-major of the British army, and by John E. Singleton, KC, an ex-captain of the British army.

The trial largely consisted of a recital by crown counsel of the 'evidence' presented at our preliminary hearings, and a recital by Mr Maden and Mr Lynskey of the 'evidence' that we had lit the fires at Hall Road.

In summing-up, the judge told the jury that they were to consider their evidence 'on the bare facts of the case as common-sense business people,' and they obliged him by finding us guilty on all counts. He then sentenced Seamus O'Malley (who was carrying a revolver when he was arrested) to ten years penal servitude, Joseph Hayes to seven years penal servitude, and Bernie Meehan, Charlie O'Gorman and I to five years penal servitude. (In a separate trial Paddy Lowe was sentenced to ten years penal servitude.)

We laughed back at the judge as he read out our sentences, and after he finished we all stood and shouted, 'Up the Republic! Up the Rebels!' before being led away to the cells beneath the court.

Before we were sent off to begin our sentences, one relative was allowed to see us, and my mother – Lord have Mercy on her! – was brought up to the iron bars by two warders, one of whom whispered a few words of consolation to her – in Irish. I got up to meet her and tried to smile and said, 'A felon's hat is the noblest crown an Irish head can wear.' She looked at me, the tears streaming down her face, and the warders led her away.

5

ONE BRIGHT, SUNNY MORNING AT Walton, not long after our trial, we were lined up in our prison uniforms and then handcuffed to a long chain. We were to be taken to Dartmoor Prison to begin our sentences of penal servitude. We were led out of Walton to a van and taken to Lime Street Station in Liverpool where we were put into a train compartment with our escorting warders. When the train pulled out of Lime Street, the warders took out their cigarettes and started to smoke. We asked them if *we* could smoke, but the bastards said no, and it was a long ride to Bristol!

The train finally pulled into Bristol Station where we were to change trains for Exeter: we were to spend the night at Exeter Prison before going on to Dartmoor Prison. There was a half-hour's wait at Bristol for the Exeter train, so we were taken to a platform waiting room which happened to be packed with people – mostly women and children. We must have been a sight; everyone stared at us in our prison uniforms and handcuffed to a long chain.

We were terribly thirsty; we hadn't had a drink since we left Walton in the morning. We asked the warders for water and someone brought us a bucket and a mug. As we crowded around the bucket, someone along the chain shouted: 'Up Sinn Féin!' and then we all started. 'Up the Republic! ... Up the Irish Republican Army! ... Ireland for Ever!' ...' The warders went mad and screamed for us to stop, but by this time we were enjoying it and *wouldn't* stop! We filled up with water and kept shouting ... 'Up Dev! ... Up De Valera! ... Up the IRA!' Then, when the warders saw we weren't going to stop, they started to usher people out of the waiting-room – but, bejasus, the people wouldn't move! – and then some of the women started crying. The warders were raging, but they couldn't get the people out, so they dragged *us* out. Of course, once we got to the platform we shouted louder than ever so that everyone could hear us. ' ... Up Sinn Féin! ... Ireland for Ever!' Then some fool in a Salvation Army uniform came over to us with a fistful of pamphlets and religious tracts

– to 'save' us! – but one of the warders chased him.

When we got to Exeter Prison, we were put in separate cells for the night. About nine o'clock next morning, we left Exeter aboard another train for Tavistock, where we were put into a van and taken across the moor. We attracted the attention of a lot of people on their way to market; they knew we were convicts on our way to Princetown and the moor's infamous prison. And what a forbidding place it looked as we got closer! Built from blocks of granite during the wars with Napoleon more than a hundred years previously, it looked a terribly lonely place in the middle of those wild moors. It even had an arch whose Latin inscription – PARCERE SUBJECTIS[29] – taunted us as we were led beneath it in a parody of an imperial triumph.

When we got inside Dartmoor Prison, we were lined up on the Reception Floor – which was the ground floor of the Punishment Block! – before we were taken to our cells in 'A' Hall and given our first meal – a mug of cocoa and a slice of bread. My cell was painted a colour I'll never forget; it was as if someone had mixed blue paint with whitewash and then smeared the walls with it. I was trying to get used to the colour and the way it had been put on the walls when a warder opened the door and threw in a book. 'Here's a book for you to read,' he said. I picked it up. It was called *Tales of Mystery and Imagination*, by Edgar Allan Poe.

The next morning we were issued with our Dartmoor Prison uniforms. First, we each got a pair of old boots – not new ones! – with quarter-inch iron studs nailed in the soles so as to form an arrowhead. Every time you walked on the ground you left a trail of arrows! We got a pair of heavy woollen stockings that came above our knees; they were black, patterned with one-inch thick red rings. Then we got a pair of khaki-coloured knickers which were fastened just below the knees with a button. Running up the front of the knickers were two rows of black arrows – each about two inches high – on each side. There was an arrow just above the knee, another one in the middle of the thigh, and a third one just below the waist. Our tunics were the same colour as the knickers but had no seams: there was one breast pocket in the tunic. The tunic had two rows of arrowheads running up the front – one on each side – and one row up the middle of the back. They gave us each a handkerchief: a big blue one with black stripes. The last item we got was a wedge-shaped forage cap, like the ones the soldiers wore in the Second World War. On the side of the cap was a number. Mine was 977.

A convict at Dartmoor was identified by the numbers and letters on his cap, the letters indicating the years of his imprisonment to hard labour.

I didn't have a letter in front of the number on my cap: none of the IRA prisoners arrested in England had letters on their caps. The IRA prisoners arrested in Ireland and brought over to Dartmoor had neither letters nor numbers on their caps. It made it easy for the prison warders to know who we were, but it also helped the IRA prisoners to recognise each other!

After we had been at Dartmoor a few days, we received an additional piece of uniform – a coverall for working in. It was a big, loose jacket with red, white, and blue stripes running all the way around. It reminded me of the sort of thing you might see on a circus clown.

Not long after I'd been in prison, I saw a poor fellow dressed in a uniform that made mine look pretty dull. He was a convict who'd tried to escape. One half of the front of his jacket was a canary yellow, the other side was khaki. When he turned around, the back of his tunic was done in the same colours as the front; one side of the back was yellow, the other side was khaki. His knickers were the same colour as his tunic: each leg was half yellow, half khaki, back and front! Around each of his ankles was an iron ring, like a bracelet: he had another couple of rings around his knees. Then there was a chain around his waist, and hanging down each side from his waist were two more chains which were fastened to the rings about his knees and then to the rings above his ankles. The poor man – God help him – had to hold the chains just above his knees if he wanted to walk. Not that he had much chance to walk anywhere – the poor fellow would spend the rest of his sentence in solitary confinement, except for his daily 'exercise' walk!

In the mornings right after breakfast we were called for our daily exercises; when the cell doors were opened, we stood in our doorways until we got the order to step forward. There was plenty of room in the doorways because the walls were two feet thick! As we lined up in two rows in the hallway, the warders would keep shouting, 'Press up! ... Press up!' until each prisoner was pressed up tightly against the man in front, and his shoulders rubbed those of the man beside him. When they had about twenty men pressed together as closely as possible, we were given the order, 'Quick march!' and we all moved off in step – otherwise someone would have toppled over! Moving like that became such a habit that you could always tell an old lag by the way he walked; when he walked, he lifted his feet and thrust them out in front, sort of sideways. When we reached the exercise yard, we were marched past the principal warder and the governor, or his deputy, with one warder in front of us and another at the back. The governor, Captain Francis Morgan,[30] stood on a big stone just like a general reviewing his troops. Whenever the deputy-governor, Major Edward French,[31] came out, I always had the feeling he enjoyed watching the IRA prisoners trudging by. He was the second son of Viscount French, the hated 'Lord Lieutenant' of Ireland.[32]

We were marched around the exercise yard in three circles, each convict about two or three paces behind the one in front. The younger men marched around in the outside ring, the middle-aged men were in the middle ring, and the oldest cons – those barely able to toddle along – moved around in the inside ring. Talking was forbidden, and the warders were posted around the yard to keep an eye on us; but we still managed to have a good chat once we learned to talk without moving our lips. After a good bit of practice when you were alone in your cell, you could speak quite easily without moving your lips. Out in the exercise yard, a warder could be looking straight at you and not see you talking! As we plodded around in the circles we heard the latest prison rumours, and passed on messages. We told each other what we were in for, how long we had been there, and so on.

Dartmoor was a prison for recidivists – hardened convicts who'd been in and out of jails all their lives; they were beyond redemption.

In the local English prisons (such as Walton) were kept first-timers; they were segregated from all other prisoners and wore a red star on their caps if they behaved themselves. When a prisoner was sentenced to penal servitude for the first time, he went to Parkhurst Prison on the Isle of Wight; if he was sentenced to penal servitude a second time, he went to Portland Prison; but if the poor devil was incorrigible, he was sent off to Dartmoor. So there we were: Volunteers of the Irish Republican Army – who'd never before seen the inside of a prison – doing penal servitude in Dartmoor Prison! But then, we weren't the first Irishmen sent to Dartmoor for fighting for Ireland; De Valera had been sent there in 1919, two years before us! It was an old tradition – going back as far as the days of Queen Elizabeth! – for the British to send the most determined of Irish nationalists to the worst prisons in England in the hope of breaking their spirit. Look at what they did to the Fenians![33] Our lads, the Liverpool Volunteers, were the first of the Volunteers to arrive in Dartmoor, but it wasn't long before we were joined by Volunteers captured in Manchester, London and Newcastle. We even had a few more from the Liverpool Company when John McPhillips, Batty Keaney, and a few others were captured.

After our capture at Hall Road, the Liverpool Company was responsible for more farm fires and the cutting down of telegraph poles in Birkenhead. They also destroyed some of the homes of Black and Tans who came from Liverpool. IRA Headquarters in Dublin had given orders for the homes of Black and Tans to be destroyed, but we didn't think much of the idea of sending Volunteers to cut down telegraph poles in Birkenhead. It seemed a reckless and futile use of the Volunteers, and we blamed the man responsible for the Hall Road job: Hughie Early.

A few days after I arrived at Dartmoor, the Catholic chaplain came to see me. His name was Fr Finnegan, a big Irish priest who said he was from Co. Cavan.[34] He told me I looked very young and asked me how old I was. I told him I was nineteen, and he asked me if I knew how to serve mass. I said yes, and that it would be an honour for me to serve; after that I was allowed out of my cell every morning to serve mass.

After mass and our morning exercises, I had to join my work party in the prison laundry. I got along very well with one of the old cons I worked with, and one day he asked me to get him a match. I asked him how the hell I was supposed to be able to get him a match when we never even saw a match or a cigarette.

'I'm a Catholic,' he said, 'and at mass on Sundays I see you lighting those bloody candles. So you get me the match, and I'll give you the butt. I have the cigarette, you get the match.'

I agreed. I'd have given my right arm for a cigarette – or even a butt!

Before mass, I always went up to the priest in the sacristy to tell him that I was ready to light the candles; then he'd take out a match – one match – and give it to me. One morning I took the match and when I got to the altar I deliberately struck the wrong end, and went back to the priest and asked him for another match telling him the first one wouldn't light. That's how I stole the match! But the problem was to somehow hide it on me and get it back to my cell.

I knew I ran the risk of being searched. Prisoners were often searched – very thoroughly; a couple of warders might just take you out of line and bring you to one of the empty cells and make you strip everything off. While you stood there completely in the nude, they went through your clothes, inch by inch. Then they made you put your feet up and searched between your toes; then they made you bend over and they looked at your backside to see if you had anything hidden in your arse.

Well, I was in a real sweat over how I was going to hide that match. But after mass I noticed the only seam in my tunic – the one along the bottom edge of my breast pocket – and with a little effort, managed to break one of the threads. Then I broke the match about three-eights of an inch below the head, and with some more effort, managed to work the match head into the seam. After another couple of weeks I pulled the same stunt again and ended up with two match heads.

The old con was delighted when I gave him his match, and a few days later he was able to give me a cigarette butt. That night I waited in my cell until the warder had checked through the observation hatch in the door and then climbed up on my planks near the vent, lit the butt and took a glorious puff. My head began to spin and I almost fell off the bed; it was months since I'd had a smoke. But, Jasus, I was in heaven!

Then one day the priest told me he wasn't going to let me serve mass anymore because I was stealing the wine. I could have gone through the floor when he accused me of stealing the altar wine. I couldn't believe that he'd think I would do a thing like that. I did smoke; I'd been smoking for two or three years before I was arrested, but I didn't drink. I'd never touched the stuff. The thought of stealing some of the altar wine had never crossed my mind.

That priest wasn't popular with the prisoners. He had no sympathy or kindness for us, particularly the Volunteers. The warders treated us better than he did. One day when the priest was making his rounds, the fellow in the next cell to me – who was also a Catholic, but not a Volunteer – whispered to me; 'The padre is coming and I'm ready for him!' He started to grin and showed me his slate. It was covered with a drawing of a nude woman!

I got to know a few of the convicts, and some of them were real characters. One of them was Clayton, a small dapper fellow and a hardened crook. He'd already served a five-year sentence and was doing a second five-year stretch. But he told everyone that he was turning over a new leaf; that crime didn't pay, and he was finished with it. He was sent to prison for impersonating an army officer and for forging cheques. He used to dress up as an army major – medals and all – and steal a car. Then he'd go to a big hotel for a few days and write out false cheques; then he'd disappear for a while, pop up in another town and do the same think all over again, until he was caught. The Protestant chaplain spent a lot of time with Clayton and was delighted the fellow was going to give up his life of crime. Clayton was able to get a lot of little favours on account of his friendship with the padre. Then he was released, but was back again within a month! As soon as he reached Plymouth he'd bought himself an army officer's uniform, but the police were waiting for him and arrested him on the spot.

Then there was West who liked to tell how famous he was; that he once rated three columns in the *News of the World*. 'And listen to this,' he'd say. 'If you go to the museum in Scotland Yard, you'll see all my tools there. They've got them in a glass case. I invented a special little auger for boring a hole through a window sash. Then I had a little wire that went through the hole and looped on the catch; all I had to do was pull on the wire, and I was in. The police said I was a bloody genius!'

I met a Harley Street doctor when I was working in the engineering shop. I was sent there from the prison laundry to work on one of the boilers that was being repaired. The fellow who worked with me on the boiler spoke with an Oxford accent, and when I remarked on this, he told me about himself. He had had a medical practice in Harley Street in London and had become very well known. When he was invited out to parties in Mayfair he learned where the jewellery was kept – and then he'd slip back later and steal it!

But the only convicts I had much pity for were the poor devils brought over from Ireland to do their penal servitude in England. They were brought over from Dublin because there wasn't enough room for them in the Irish prisons which were filled with IRA men. One of the convicts who arrived from Dublin was a fellow by the name of O'Carroll who'd robbed – or tried to rob – a post office with a revolver, posing as an IRA man. I remember him because I was working in the prison cookhouse at the time, and he was being given special meals on account of his bad stomach. The prison doctor had transferred him to the hospital ward for two or three days, and then sent the poor man back to his cell saying he was cured.

The Irish convicts taken over from Dublin were treated the same as the English convicts; they weren't allowed to go near the IRA prisoners brought over from Ireland. One of the poor devils, who was given penal servitude for repeatedly stealing bicycles, was in a cell not far from mine. Prison life got him down so much I often heard him in the middle of the night saying his rosary.

Although the IRA prisoners were a distinct group – and were identified as such by the omission of letters from our caps – the prison authorities in Dartmoor persisted in treating us as habitual criminals. Some of us in 'A' Hall agreed that we should demand to be treated as political prisoners and that we should go on strike to back up that demand. All the Volunteers in 'A' Hall (that is, all those arrested in England) were canvassed for their opinion and they all agreed to join in a work strike. We set a date for the strike to begin and word was passed to the IRA prisoners in 'D' Hall (those Volunteers arrested in Ireland) telling them what we planned to do and asking for their support. On the day for the strike to begin, most of the Volunteers were good to their word and refused to join the labour gangs, but when some weakened at the last moment and went to work as usual, the strike soon collapsed.

Those of us who'd refused to go to work were given three days on bread and water, but the punishment had two effects which the prison authorities hadn't foreseen. First, it made those of us who'd participated in the strike more determined than ever to be recognised as political prisoners; and second, it shamed those who had weakened the first time into being resolute the next time we went on strike.

Shortly after the collapse of the first work strike, several of us planned a second work strike, and when we were sure of better support from the Volunteers in both 'A' and 'D' Halls, we set a date for the start of the second strike. This time the strike was more successful, but once again some Volunteers went back on their word and let us down.

When I refused to leave my cell for work the day the second strike began, two warders grabbed me and hauled me up before the prison governor who charged me with refusing to work. 'Isolation cells,' he barked. 'Three days Punishment Diet No. 1; fourteen days Punishment Diet No. 2.'

I was then escorted downstairs and thrown into a darkened cell lit only by the daylight which filtered through a small, grimy windowpane near the ceiling. In the dim light I saw that the cell was bare of all furniture and fittings except for a table and a bed. The 'table' was a round block of wood – just like a tree stump – fixed into the floor close to the door, and the 'bed' consisted of three narrow wooden planks set into the floor's tarred surface.

At night time, a warder opened the cell door and in exchange for all my clothes which he booted into the corridor, threw me a blanket. I had a difficult time trying to get to sleep because I had no pillow, and when I lay down on my 'bed' with the banket wrapped tightly around me, the planks – which were several inches apart from each other – dug into me.

In the morning the cell door was opened by a warder who took the blanket away and booted my clothes back into the cell. Accompanying the warder was a trustee carrying a basin of cold water, a piece of soap, and a towel, but I'd no sooner dipped my hands into the basin than it was snatched away and the cell door was slammed shut. Later each morning the governor or the deputy-governor came to inspect the prisoners in the isolation cells. The cell doors were opened in turn as the governor came along the corridor, and as he passed each cell he shouted, 'Awright?' but before one could answer, the door was slammed shut.

Every prisoner in the isolation cells was given up to an hour of 'exercise' each day. The prisoner was escorted to any one of a number of exercise yards used exclusively by prisoners in the isolation cells. The 'yards' weren't much larger than the cells and had ten or twelve-foot high walls on three sides and a row of iron bars the same height on the fourth side which contained a gate leading into the yard. Once inside the yard, I had to walk in a circle the whole time I was there, while the warder kept watch on me from the other side of the gate. For me it was like being in a bear pit or a cage at the zoo.

While I was on Punishment Diet No. 1, I was fed a two-inch cube of hard bread and a beaker of water – three times a day. Then, for the next fourteen days when I was in Punishment Diet No. 2, I was given a bowl of skilly – a thin porridge or gruel with a piece or two of potato floating in it – at dinner time, in addition to the bread and water.

If the prison authorities believed they had taught us a lesson, they were badly mistaken, because as soon as we were released from our fourteen days of isolation, Paddy Lowe and I decided that we'd carry on the fight for recognition as political prisoners one step further – we'd go on a hunger strike; we'd take the bread and water but no other food. We passed the word along to the other IRA prisoners in both 'A' and 'D' Halls and invited anyone who wished to do so, to join us. All the Volunteers in 'A' Hall agreed to go on hunger strike with us, but we wouldn't allow Seán O'Byrne, a Volunteer from the Liverpool Company who offered to join us, to take part. He had a withered hand, and God knows, it was affliction enough for the poor fellow.

When the hunger strike began we refused to eat the meals (except for the bread and water) brought to us. The warders tried everything they could think of in order to get us to eat – they even slid the meals through hatches in the cell doors, closing the hatches before we could push the food back out again.

On the eleventh or twelfth day of the hunger strike, a priest – not our regular chaplain, Fr Finnegan – came to see us in an effort to persuade us to give it up. Unlike Fr Finnegan, the visiting priest was a gentle, kind-looking man and, wearing the Benedictine habit, was the very picture of a saintly old monk.[35] None of us knew anything about him, but the rumour was that he was from Buckfast Abbey, only about ten miles or so from the prison. He asked us if we had an officer, and I said that the commandant of the Volunteers in 'D' Hall was our commandant too.

This 'monk' advised us to give up the strike, but we told him we wouldn't accept his advice; we demanded to be treated as political prisoners, not as criminals or convicts. The 'monk' said he'd go over to 'D' Hall and talk to the commandant there, and we told him to tell the men in 'D' Hall that we thought they should be giving us more support – to the end. Well, the 'monk' ran back and forth between our block and 'D' Hall trying to get us to give up the strike, and finally he came to me and said, 'Will you obey an order from your officer?' I told him I was a soldier in the Irish Republican Army, and that as a soldier, I'd obey my officers. He returned after a while and said,

'I have a direct order from your commanding officer: you are to come off this strike.' I asked him the officer's name, but I don't think he knew it. I told him to go and see Paddy Lowe, because I knew that the two of us were in this together to the bitter end. We either came off the strike together, or we would keep it up together. Finally Paddy and I agreed we'd come off the strike; but we told the 'monk' to tell the governor that the only reason we were giving up the strike was that we were obeying an order from one of our officers to do so.

But, by God, we were as weak as kittens! For a week we'd had nothing but bread and water, and for about the last four days we had taken *neither* bread *nor* water! Paddy Lowe told me I looked like a skeleton – and I told him *he* did!

A terrible bitterness lingered among the Volunteers long after that hunger strike. For a long time I wouldn't speak to the lads such as John McPhillips and Batty Keaney who refused to join us in both the work strikes and the hunger strike. Eventually I got over it. I came to realise that you can't blame a man if he hasn't got the courage to go through with something like that. Some men are made of steel, others are made of brass – and you can't expect a piece of brass to act like steel. It's as simple as that. I saw it during the Civil War in Ireland; I saw it during the Spanish Civil War; and I saw it on the ships in the Second World War.

But the bitterness was never forgotten by some of us. Johnny MacAlinden – Lord have Mercy on him! – was one of the greatest friends I ever had; he was an apprenticed brass-finisher in Newcastle at the time he was arrested for Volunteer activities. Just before he died a few years ago, I used to drop in to see him and try to cheer him up by telling him we'd be knocking back a few pints as soon as he was on his feet again. During one of the last times I saw him, he said to me, 'Ah, Seán, will you do one last thing for me when I'm gone? Will you put the flag over me?'

'Don't you know well that I will?' I replied. 'Weren't we in Dartmoor together? Didn't we go through the Civil War together?'

We went on to talk about old times, and then he said to me, 'Do you remember the strikes?'

'I do,' I said.

'Do you remember Eoin Salmon?' he asked.

'Indeed I do,' I said. He and Eoin had been together in the Newcastle Company of the IRA until they were arrested and brought to Dartmoor. After they were released and went to Dublin, Eoin joined the Garda Síochána – the Civic Guard – when it was formed at the Curragh to take over from the Royal Irish Constabulary and the Dublin Metropolitan Police.

'You know I didn't take part in the strikes, ' said Johnny.

'Oh, forget it!' I said.

'It's just this,' he said. 'I feel badly about Eoin, because we'd always been such good friends until the strikes. But you know, Seán, he never spoke a word to me from the day of those strikes until the day he died. I often passed him on the streets here, when he was in the gardaí, but he never spoke to me.'

Eoin – God rest him – took part in the work strikes but not the hunger strike.

When the strike was over, I managed one morning to have a brief chat in the sacristy with Seamus Devins, the commandant of the Volunteers in 'D' Hall. Seamus, who took care of the sacristy and played the harmonium at mass on Sundays, was Mayor of Sligo, a deputy in the 'illegal' Dáil Éireann and a brigadier-general in the IRA. I asked him why so many of the men in 'D' Hall hadn't supported us in the strikes, and I told him that when the prison authorities saw so many of them back out, they knew we weren't united. Then he told me that most of the men in 'D' Hall weren't IRA men at all! They'd been rounded up in Ireland merely on suspicion; they were *sympathetic* to the nationalist movement – but that was all. He also told me that many of the Volunteers in 'D' Hall were 'Trucers' – men who joined the IRA after the Anglo-Irish Truce came into effect (on 11 July 1921).

Our conversation was cut short by the approach of Fr Finnegan, but I had another opportunity to talk to Seamus Devins shortly before he was released to take part in the Dáil discussions on Lloyd George's proposals for an Anglo-Irish treaty. Although none of us knew the details of the proposals, it was generally believed that while they offered a large measure of political independence for Ireland, they fell short of our expectations for a completely independent republic embracing all of Ireland.

'Why must we accept the British terms for a treaty?' I asked Seamus more out of curiosity than disappointment.

'Seán,' he said, 'we've got to accept. We must sign a treaty ... we're almost finished ... there's hardly anyone left to carry on the fight. At the rate the Tans are arresting us you can imagine what it will be like within twelve months if we don't accept. We don't have much choice ... it's the best we can do.'

I asked him to call on my mother as he passed through Liverpool on his way to Dublin and tell her I was all right, and he promised that he would. We shook hands and said goodbye to each other in the sacristy and that was the last time I saw him.

He was unable to call on my mother because he went directly to Holyhead where he caught a boat for Dublin, but before he sailed from Holyhead he sent her a note assuring her I was all right.

Later, when I was released from Dartmoor, I was surprised when I learned that Seamus had voted in the Dáil against the acceptance of the Treaty. Then, during the subsequent Civil War, I read in a newspaper one day that Seamus Devins, together with his divisional adjutant, Bryan MacNeill,[36] and three others had been killed on Benbulbin Mountain (in Co. Sligo) on Wednesday 20 September 1922 by a party of troops under Seán MacEoin.

I was particularly saddened when I read of Seamus' death because I remembered him best as the organist for the Catholic chapel in Dartmoor Prison. At the end of Sunday mass, Seamus always played the hauntingly beautiful strains of 'The Coolin'[37] an ancient Gaelic melody that had survived the suppression of Irish culture during the time of the Penal Laws. The significance of that symbolic piece of music being played for us was lost, of course, on the stolid warders guarding us at mass, but it wasn't lost on us!

The day the Anglo-Irish Treaty was signed – Tuesday 6 December 1921 – the word somehow reached the men in 'D' Hall that Ireland's War of Independence was over, and they all went wild!

Pandemonium broke out: everyone was shouting, cheering, and singing. Some of them sang rebel songs and some of them sang hymns. Later in the night when most of the noise died down, we could hear some of them saying the rosary together. The noise of the men going wild for joy must have been heard in Princetown! The warders tried to stop it, of course; they went into a few of the noisier cells and batoned the lads inside them.

The next morning as we were going around on our exercise 'walk,' we suddenly saw a group of warders dragging one of the men from 'D' Hall through the exercise yard on the way to the Punishment Block. As they dragged him along, the warders kept clubbing him until he went as limp as a rag doll. It was too much for us; Paddy Lowe and I left our places in the circle and dashed across to help the poor fellow being beaten to a pulp. But the moment we left our places, the warders guarding us drew their batons and ran over to block us. We fought like terriers, and somehow I managed to break away and ran for the gate leading to 'D' Hall. I had hoped to reach the lads in 'D' Hall to tell them what was being done to one of their comrades.

I ran like a deer and headed straight for the gate in the wall, but the gate guard stepped out in front of me and threw his rifle to his shoulder. 'Halt!' he shouted. 'Halt, or I'll fire!' I saw that I didn't have a chance; he was only a few feet ahead of me and had me covered. I stopped and raised my arms. I knew he'd riddle me if I gave him the slightest excuse. Nothing would have pleased him more! But before I knew it, I was surrounded by warders and getting the beating of my life: batons, boots, fists – the whole bloody lot. When they finally had me trussed up, they began to drag *me* to the Punishment Block! One of the bastards managed to get my wrists locked behind my back and was saying to the others, 'Break his arms! ... break the son-of-a-bitch's arms!' until one of the warders, a little fair-haired man with a moustache, pulled him away and said, 'Don't do that! ... he'll be all right! ... he's coming quietly!' As soon as they got me to the door of the Punishment Block, the other warders went off and left the little fair-haired warder to take me inside. 'Come quietly!' he said, 'and for

God's sake son, don't speak a word. No matter what they do, don't speak a word.'

The little fair-haired warder was a Catholic. I remembered seeing him at the altar rail in the prison chapel when he came up for Holy Communion.

When we got inside the iron gate of the Punishment Block, another lot of warders took over, and they led me to the centre of the ground floor where there was a stairwell leading down to punishment cells on the floor below. The iron staircase looked very much like the stairways in a ship's engine room, with just enough room for one man to go up or down, and steep enough that you had to hang on to the handrail. We were at the top of the staircase and I was looking down to where four warders were waiting at the bottom, when one of them shouted, 'Throw him down!' – and I was flung head over heels down the stairs to the warders at the bottom. When I rolled off the last step, they met me with their boots, mercilessly. I tried to cover my head with my arms, but they kicked the shite out of me. When they finished with me I was nothing but blood from head to toe, and when they threw me in the cell I just lay on the floor thinking I was dying. I crawled close to one of the walls and made an act of contrition.

The next thing I remember was a foot on my shoulder and someone telling me to stand up. I looked up, and there was the prison doctor and one of the orderlies from the hospital. I tried to get on my feet but fell back to the floor.

Then I heard the doctor saying to the orderly, 'Get him upstairs to the hospital ward, quick!'

After five days in the prison hospital – which was like a very large cell except that it had proper beds instead of the usual wooden planks – I was taken out into the corridor where the doctor sat at a little table. He looked me over, and the warder beside him said, 'Ah, two black eyes!'

The doctor turned around to him and said, 'Shut up! And take him away. Back to the punishment cells and finish your seventeen days.'

That's when I learned what my punishment was: seventeen days of solitary confinement on a diet of bread and water!

When my seventeen days in solitary were over, I was taken before the governor.

'We are sending you to Swansea Prison,' he said. 'You will be isolated from your so-called comrades ... you will not see them again. You will be taken to Swansea Prison, and I know it's a damned rough place ... you know what the food is like in the local prisons, don't you? ...'

I remembered the food we had in Walton, and had heard that food in the other local prisons was no better.

The governor looked at me, waiting for a reply. I just shrugged my shoulders.

'You have lost all privileges and remission of your sentence,' he said. 'Dismissed! ... March him away!'

When I was returned to my old cell, I learned that Paddy Lowe had also been beaten up and batoned at the time I got my clattering. Although he didn't end up in the hospital ward, he, too, got seventeen days of solitary confinement on bread and water.

The priest, Fr Finnegan, came around to see me soon after I was released from the punishment cells. I told him I'd made an act of contrition when I thought I was dying after the beating I got. I said I thought I should go to confession because at school we'd been told that if we made an act of contrition when we were in danger of death, our sins would be forgiven, but that we had a solemn obligation to go to confession to a priest as soon as possible afterwards.

The priest looked at me for a moment, scornfully, and then started to snicker.

'O my God!' I said to myself. 'And him a priest! ... an Irish Catholic priest!' My heart nearly broke.

The Irish prisoners in 'D' Hall were eventually released in January (1922), as a result of the General Amnesty which had been drawn up by Eamonn Duggan. Duggan, a member of the Irish delegation which signed the Anglo-Irish Treaty, had also asked for the release of the Irish prisoners who had been convicted in England and Scotland, but we were kept back because Lloyd George wanted us as hostages for the Treaty.

When the men from 'D' Hall were released from their cells, they paraded in one of the exercise yards and demanded that the governor come and see them; they told him they refused to leave unless their comrades arrested in England were allowed to go with them. But the governor told them there was nothing he could do about it.

So those of us arrested in England were kept until two or three weeks later, when suddenly, on 14 February – St Valentine's Day! – we were taken from our cells and told we were going out. It wasn't until we reached Liverpool that I found out the circumstances that led to our sudden and unexpected release. When Neill Kerr learned that we had not been released with the prisoners arrested in Ireland, he immediately went to see Mick Collins and told him about it, and Collins personally demanded our release from the British authorities. And yet, when the 'split' came, some of our lads actually fought against Collins!

When we left Dartmoor Prison, the authorities wouldn't let old John Fitzgerald come with us. He was seventy years old, but they wouldn't let him go. I believe it was because he'd been arrested during the Truce. Old John boarded with the Healys on Rimrose Road, Bootle, near the Labour Exchange. Healy and his eldest son were Corkonians who worked as firemen on the boats going from Liverpool to Cork, and the police suspected Healy's place as being an arms dump, which it was! They were going to arrest Healy, a married man with children, but old John Fitzgerald – a member of the IRB and one of the greatest Fenians that ever lived in Liverpool – spoke up and took the blame; he said *he* was responsible for the arms found in the house and was sentenced to ten years penal servitude. Of course he *wasn't* responsible, but he couldn't bear seeing Healy, the father of those children, taken off to prison.

When he was a young man – the way I heard it – John became involved in the Fenian movement and decided to dedicate his live to Irish freedom, like a priest dedicating his life to God and the Church. John wouldn't marry: he wanted to devote his life to Ireland.

Whenever I met him in Dartmoor, he always gave me a big smile. When I passed his cell with the food trolley, I always tried to throw him an extra piece of cheese. We all did. I know Bernie Meehan did, because we worked together trying to steal that extra piece of cheese.

Before we left Dartmoor Prison we were all brought out into one of the yards, and one of us – I don't know who he was – gave the order, 'Fall in!' and we all lined up in three ranks. Someone shouted, 'Quick march!' and we marched – yes, *marched* – to the gates saying, 'We came here as soldiers of the IRA, and by God we'll leave as soldiers of the IRA! We'll show these bastards!' The bloody warders just looked at us; they didn't know what to make of us, I'm sure. When we got to the gates we halted, and shouted: 'We want John Fitzgerald out! ... We want John Fitzgerald out!'

The governor came down to see us and said. 'That is a matter between your government and mine ... there is nothing I can do ... I cannot let him go with you ... it is a matter between your government and mine. I must act under *my* orders; you must act under *your* orders.'

But eventually he did get out some months later, and went straight across to Ireland. How old John must have looked forward to returning to Ireland, now free and independent! Well, someone gave him a job – a dirty, menial one – in Portobello barracks. I'm sure that brave old Fenian's heart must have broken. In three weeks he was dead.

There was nothing more we could do, so we marched out, and two very old warders escorted us to the railway station. The two old screws had been deliberately chosen to escort us, because we had never seen them before. When we arrived at the station we did a bit of drill and then marched onto the platform. We were all desperate for a smoke, and I went up to the engine driver who was smoking a cigarette and said, 'Would you give an old lag a cigarette?' and he pulled out a package of Woodbines and gave me one.

We all piled into one of the compartments on the waiting train, and hooted the two old warders, who took off, running for dear life. We thought it very funny to see them running like that, as if they were afraid we'd go for them.

When the train got to Plymouth, we sent a telegram to the crowd in Liverpool telling them we'd be arriving at Lime Street Station in Liverpool at – let us say, 7.30pm that evening – I've forgotten the exact time. But someone in the telegraph office deliberately altered the time to an hour later, so our families and friends in Liverpool did not expect us until, say, 8.30pm.

But when we arrived, some people had already begun to gather at Lime Street Station to welcome us back. Tom Kerr was there. When we stepped off the train, he was the first to meet us. Good old Tom! We formed a line on the platform, came to attention and saluted him, and he returned the salute. We all marched out of the station together – the police were there, but they didn't say a word – and we went to No. 93 Scotland Road. When we got to Scotland Road, whom did we see but Jimmy Lowe leading the Patrick Pearse Pipers Band marching towards the station to meet us!

When we arrived at No. 93 there was a big spread of food waiting for us and we dived into it – the first decent food we had had since we were arrested. But we were all trembling like leaves: the excitement and the relief after those months in Dartmoor was almost too much for us. When I got home, I couldn't sleep in my bed that night, I was so used to the hard planks in the prison. The next morning my mother found me asleep on the floor.

6

HAVING SPENT A FEW DAYS with our relatives and friends in Liverpool, those of us who'd been released from Dartmoor decided to go to Dublin together. Now that Ireland was independent, we wanted to live and work there. There was still considerable hostility against us in England, and Liverpool was no place for us who'd done so much damage to its docks, warehouses, timber yards, and surrounding farms.

When we arrived in Dublin, the White Cross representatives were there to meet us and they sent us over to Barry's Hotel, a noted IRA hangout in Great Denmark Street. The White Cross paid our bills for food and lodging, and gave us some pocket money so that we'd have a chance to get on our feet again and find ourselves jobs.

Someone told me I could probably get a job at the Broadstone Railway Station, because fitters were needed in the railway workshops there. Countess Markievicz[38] had sent word over to Barry's Hotel that she'd like to meet some of those who had recently been released from Dartmoor Prison, and that she might be able to help them get a job, so I decided to go and see her.

The Countess had an office in Dame Street, opposite the Bank of Ireland. When I met her, she asked me about Liverpool and the activities of the Liverpool Company of the Volunteers. We also talked about trade unions. When I told her I was a fitter and was hoping to get job at the Broadstone, she said that she wanted to see all of us getting back into ordinary life again, and she'd see to it that I got the job. 'Don't worry about the apprenticeship,' she said. 'Don't worry about a thing. I'll get you started at the Broadstone. You'll be back at your trade as a fitter. We'll take care of everything ... we're only too glad to have you on account of what you've done for the country.'

She gave me a note of introduction to give to the secretary of the Irish Engineering Union who was a friend of hers. The fellow lived in either Gardiner Row or Gardiner Place and when I gave him the note from the Countess he shook hands with me. 'Whatever the Countess says is good enough for me,' he said.

I started working at the Broadstone and continued living at Barry's Hotel – they were the best of people and the food was good – but the atmosphere of the place was getting us down. It had too much of that drab cheerlessness that was – and still is – typical of a Dublin guest house.

On the following Sunday afternoon we were all walking together down Sackville Street (now O'Connell Street) when we met a fellow named Fox whom some of the lads knew. His only son – a young lad in his teens – had been killed in St Stephen's Green during the Rising and he was still heartbroken over the loss of the boy.

When he heard we were dissatisfied with Barry's Hotel he invited us over to where he was staying to see if his landlady, Mrs O'Riordan, could squeeze us into her house in North Portland Place. We said we didn't mind being a bit crowded so long as we could stay together. His landlady put us all into the basement rooms of her big house, and with the fires roaring in the grates we were as happy as kings.

One night after tea at Mrs O'Riordan's we were talking about the Irish army which was being formed. We'd already seen a few of the soldiers in their green uniforms and when someone suggested we should all join up together it sounded like a great idea. We agreed that since Ireland was building a real army of its own we who had been Volunteers should be among the first to join it.

Then Seamus O'Malley, who hadn't been home to Oughterard in years, said he'd like to see his mother again before joining the army, and we all went down to Kingsbridge Station to see him off. Just before his train pulled out he told us he'd be back within a week, and that if we joined the army before his return to Dublin to be sure to keep a place for him in whatever company we joined. That, I'm afraid, was the last time we saw Seamus O'Malley, Lord have Mercy on him! Some months later – during the Civil War – I opened a newspaper one day and read that Seamus had been executed in Tuam, Co. Galway, for carrying a gun. He'd joined the anti-Treatyites and had been captured by someone on our side.

After Seamus O'Malley left us, Joseph Hayes said he was interested in joining the Garda Síochána (or Civic Guard as it was popularly called), the police force then being organised to replace the RIC. He'd been told to make further enquiries at Curragh Camp. When we saw him off on the train one morning, he said he'd be back again that night. But that was the last time any of us saw Edward Joseph Hayes. Over the years several of us tried to trace him, but without success. We asked for him at his home in Broadford, Co. Clare, and even enquired at his former boarding house in Liverpool, but it seems as if he vanished from the face of the earth the day he went to the Curragh.

With the departure of Seamus O'Malley and Joseph Hayes, our little group broke up and each of us went his own way. I had decided to join the army and went to Beggar's Bush barracks in Dublin.

The Treaty between Ireland and England which had been signed in London on 6 December 1921, was ratified by the Dáil Éireann on 7 January 1922, by sixty-four votes to fifty-seven, a majority of only seven votes. The debate on Arthur Griffith's motion to ratify the Treaty had been extremely bitter and when the votes were finally counted it was obvious that the Dáil was badly split into two factions, pro-Treaty and anti-Treaty. To make matters worse, the IRA and its leaders were also split along pro- and anti-Treaty lines – a dreadful omen of an Irish Civil War. But as the debate on the acceptance of the Treaty raged within the Dáil, it became increasingly clear that most of the Irish people were willing to accept the Treaty which would establish the Irish Free State. The Black and Tan war had exhausted the nation, and the slender resources of the IRA were almost depleted.

On paper, at least, the strength of the IRA was impressive; but in fact most of its members had never been in action of any sort. Many units had no firearms, except perhaps for a few old shotguns, the odd rifle or carbine and, if they were fortunate, a couple of revolvers. Ammunition was so scarce that it could rarely be used for firing practice. Apart from the Dublin Brigade and a few scattered flying columns[39] which kept up a constant guerrilla warfare against the British forces, most IRA activity in Ireland had been reduced to occasional forays. At the time of the Truce, many of the most active IRA Volunteers had already been rounded up by the Black and Tans and interned.

After the Truce came into effect on 11 July 1921, thousands of men – subsequently known as 'Trucers' – had swollen the ranks of the IRA hoping to bask in the reflected glory of braver men who had fought the Black and Tans. Most of the Trucers were a gutless lot, but they proclaimed themselves as anti-Treaty and bragged openly that they were ready to die for an Irish Republic – never expecting that their bluff might be called. The Trucers became a curse on the country and in a number of irresponsible incidents threatened to upset the still hazardous relationship between Ireland and England. Worse yet, their numbers led the leadership of the anti-Treaty faction both in the Dáil and in the IRA into believing that they had an army with which they could forcibly oppose the Treaty.

The Treaty had, nevertheless, been duly ratified by the Dáil, and in accordance with the provisions of the Treaty, a 'Parliament of Southern Ireland' met in Dublin on 14 January 1922, to elect a Provisional Government to whom the British authorities were to transfer the administrative apparatus for governing the country. Michael Collins was elected Chairman of the Provisional Government and immediately set about taking over the reins of administrative control from the British. On 16 January Collins and his ministers went to Dublin Castle, for centuries the seat of British power in Ireland, and took over. Unfortunately, most of the British administrators were allowed to remain in their posts. Many of them were ex-British army personnel, and for many years afterwards they regularly held an Armistice commemoration ceremony on 11 November in the castle yard!

The first British army barracks in Dublin to be handed over to the Provisional Government was Beggar's Bush barracks, headquarters of the hated Auxiliaries.[40] Michael Collins decided to establish the headquarters of the National Army of the Irish Free State at Beggar's Bush barracks, and by 31 January 1922, the nucleus of the army was formed there when it was occupied by a small force of the Dublin Guard led by Captain Paddy Daly.[41] Enlistment for the National Army began in February, and on 1 March 1922 I entered Beggar's Bush barracks and joined up. Anyone wishing to join the National Army had to have served in the Volunteers and upon joining was, in fact, transferred from the IRA into the National Army. Contrary to anti-Treatyite propaganda, which claimed that Michael Collins and the Provisional Government of the Irish Free State were 'recruiting' an army, open recruitment for the National Army did not begin until after the Civil War had broken out.

I told an officer whom I found in the orderly room that I wanted to join the army, that I had been a volunteer in the Liverpool Company of the IRA, that I was recently released from Dartmoor Prison where I had been sentenced to five years penal servitude for IRA activity, and that Neill Kerr (who was then in Dublin) could verify my record. The officer gave me a form to sign, after which I was handed a rifle and told to take it and my small suitcase of personal belongings to one of the barrack rooms where I was to be billeted.

My first impression of Beggar's Bush barracks was that almost everything about it appeared lackadaisical. None of the recently recruited soldiers, including myself, was provided with a uniform. In fact, only a mere handful of soldiers in the barracks were fully uniformed; many of the rest were dressed partly in uniform and partly in civilian clothes.

Hughie Early had been hanging around the barracks before I got there. When asked what he was waiting for, he said that he was waiting for an army commission, but when, after three weeks, he hadn't received his commission he went to the Four Courts and threw in his lot with the anti-Treatyites. As Paddy Lawson, a member of the Dublin Guard, said to me: 'He wasn't a "Pioneer" for very long!'

Two days after I had enlisted we were all mustered outside our barracks and an officer lined us up into some sort of order. Then he addressed us and said that he wanted one of us – preferably someone who'd been an officer in the Volunteers – to be our NCO and show us how to do drill. No one stepped forward, but some of the lads spoke up and said that Seán Hunter had been in the British army and would know how to instruct us in drill.

'All right, Seán,' said the officer. 'You can take over. Give them some rifle drill.'

Seán Hunter stepped out and told us to 'Order arms!', but there was so much confusion among us that it was obvious he'd have to start at the beginning and teach us the rudiments of rifle drill. The officer who'd been watching us was evidently impressed with Seán because after the drill session he said to him, 'You'll do, Seán. You can be the NCO.'

We must have been the keenest recruits any army ever had. As awkward as we were, we were so enthusiastic that we even practised our drill during the evenings in our barrack rooms. We wanted to be good soldiers. We were proud to belong to Ireland's army and wanted the Irish people to be proud of us.

Although we hadn't yet learned the proper drill for mounting guard, several of us were posted on sentry duty around the barracks every night. One night one of the lads was found asleep at his post by the orderly officer making his rounds. The officer snatched the rifle from the sleeping soldier and then woke him up. 'I've got your rifle,' said the officer, 'and I'm going to see that you're punished for going to sleep on duty.'

'You'll do nothing of the sort,' replied the bold lad. 'Give me back my rifle!'

'I'll not,' said the officer.

The lad then pulled a No. 5 Mills bomb from out of his coat pocket and threatened to throw the grenade at the officer unless he gave him back his rifle. The officer, knowing the lad had been a member of the Active Service Unit, believed that the lad might carry out his threat and handed back the rifle. No more was said about the matter. Many of the men in the barracks still carried their own revolvers – several still had a grenade or two – from the time when they were in the IRA, and they refused to part with them.

Eventually we were formed into two companies, 'A' and 'B', which constituted the first battalion of the Dublin Guards Brigade. I found myself in 'A' Company, along with Paddy Lowe who had joined the National Army the same day I did. The captain of our company was Paddy Daly, and our lieutenant was Joe Leonard. Paddy Daly had been second-in-command of Mick Collins' Squad and had led the ambush on Lord French at Ashtown Cross in December, 1919. Joe Leonard was a member of the Squad and had taken part in the ambush on French. Later, in May, 1921, he led the heroic attempt to release Commandant Seán MacEoin from Mountjoy Prison.

Morale in our two companies was very high largely because almost all of us had seen active service in the IRA prior to the Truce. We were also very proud to be designated the Dublin Guards Brigade. Shortly before the Truce, the Active Service Unit and the Squad had been combined into a single unit known simply as 'the Guard.' Renamed 'the Dublin Guard' when it took over control of Beggar's Bush barracks from the British, its members nicknamed themselves 'the Pioneers' and formed the nucleus of the Dublin Guards Brigade.

Most of us were still without uniforms, however, when one day both companies were ordered to 'Fall in!' with our rifles outside the barracks. A military band appeared and our two companies – each about seventy-five men – marched behind it through O'Connell Street before going to the station where a train was waiting to take us to Kilkenny. But when we reached the General Post Office the band struck up 'The Red Flag'! Some of us gave a cheer, and after some laughter in the ranks, we all joined in singing the chorus:

> Though cowards flinch and traitors sneer,
> We'll keep the red flag flying here.

Jasus! How I wished James Connolly might have been there!

When we arrived at the military barracks in Kilkenny, we found that it had already been handed over to the Irish government and that the British troops were gone. As we marched into the barracks we noticed that the flag pole had been cut down. It was a petty thing for the British to have done, but it indicated how bitter they must have felt when they left.

The only other unit sharing the barracks with us was a Co. Wexford flying column of the IRA, but there was virtually no contact between our two units. We occupied separate quarters within the barracks and were assigned different duties. While the Wexford unit was given responsibility for guarding the south gate of the barracks, we guarded the main gate. The commandant of Kilkenny barracks was John T. Prout, an ex-officer of the US army who was later to become commanding officer of Waterford Command with his HQ at Clonmel. The commandant's adjutant was Heaslip, an ex-officer of the British army.

As we settled down to the routine of garrison duty, we of the Dublin Guards spent a considerable amount of our time perfecting our rifle drill. We didn't mind doing so much drill, but the lads soon began to express their disappointment that Ireland's National Army was already adopting many of the practices and traditions of the British army. We developed the distinctive ceremonial drill of the Irish military funeral,[42] but other innovations in our drill were quashed. We couldn't help noticing that some of the newly appointed officers of the National Army were rapidly succumbing to shoneenism, the slavish adoption of English manners and attitudes.

Our most immediate complaints, however, concerned the food and the lack of uniforms. The food was rotten. Many of the lads said they'd eaten better meals when they were 'on the run' from the Black and Tans. As bad as the food was, however, it was our lack of uniforms that brought matters to a head. The army had not supplied us with boots and we were still wearing our civilian boots and shoes. Almost everyone's footwear had been worn through the soles and our feet were getting wet when it rained. So few of us had overcoats that when we were assigned to do night guard duty those of us who didn't have our own overcoats had to borrow ones from the lads who'd already gone to bed for the night!

We became so dissatisfied that one morning after breakfast the lads in our company held a meeting and decided not to do any more drill until we were given uniforms and better food. That afternoon, when we were assembled on the parade ground and a sergeant gave us the order to come to attention, we remained at ease, refusing to obey him. He did everything he could think of to get us to move, but no one budged an inch. 'All right!' he said when he finally gave up. 'You're in for it! Dismiss!'

When we got back to our barrack room we held a meeting to

elect a spokesman who would represent us and take our complaint before the officers. Two of us were nominated: O'Connor (a fellow from Kerry) and myself. A vote was held and I was elected. 'Right, boys!' I said, and went straight over to the adjutant and a group of officers and told them that 'A' Company had held a meeting and decided not to do any more drill until we got uniforms and better food.

One of the officers said it was a mutiny and I said I didn't care what it was called but unless we were given food that was fit to eat we would not drill. Another officer said he was sorry if the food was that bad but that he was just a new officer. I told him that I didn't care who was new or who was old so long as we got better food. Then someone else said that we shouldn't complain because the meals were being prepared by lads like ourselves!

I also told them that we needed uniforms because our civilian clothes were wearing out. I pointed out that few of us had overcoats and that if we were caught in the rain we got soaked to the skin; I told them that some of the lads had holes in the knees and seats of their trousers and were ashamed to walk down the streets of Kilkenny because the girls were laughing at their appearance. I also told them that some of us had holes worn through the soles of our boots – our *own* boots – and that we needed new ones. 'Don't forget,' I said to Adjutant Heaslip – whose brother was a Volunteer in our company – 'we're not a bunch of corner boys; we weren't selling newspapers on the streets before we joined the army.'

I'd no sooner reported back to the lads in 'A' Company than there was a sudden commotion in the square and we looked outside to see a party of Volunteers from 'B' Company with fixed bayonets being ordered to get us out of the barracks. When 'B' Company was ordered to drive us out, Eddie Flood (Tom Flood's brother and a Volunteer in 'B' Company) got up on a table and made a speech calling on his comrades to support us. Some of the lads in 'B' Company refused to leave their barrack rooms but most of them came along and drove us – at bayonet point – towards the gymnasium. We called the escort every dirty name we could think of, but they just laughed at us as they locked us inside the gym and mounted guard on us.

We were then more determined than ever not to drill until we were given complete uniforms and better food, and when an officer came to ask us to change our minds about the strike, we repeated our demands. In the evening we were allowed out of the gymnasium to return to our barracks for the night and in the morning we were fed a huge breakfast. No attempt was made to return us to the gym and we sat around in the barrack room until dinner time. Then we heard a rumour that a couple of officers had suggested I be court-martialled and shot, but that one of the lads in 'B' Company had warned an officer that if I was shot every officer in the barracks would be shot.

When we went for dinner we were given the best meal we'd had since our arrival in Kilkenny and we discovered that 'B' Company had been taken out for a march around the town. After dinner Joe Leonard told us to assemble on the square, and when we did so he gave us a dressing-down. He said that steps had been taken to improve the meals and to provide us with complete uniforms and new boots, but that we all were to write him letters of apology or we'd be 'in for it.'

There was an immediate improvement in the food and we were soon outfitted with complete uniforms and boots, but I still hadn't written a letter of apology when Joe Leonard called me into his office a few days after the strike. He said I was the only one who hadn't written an apology and, covering the signatures, he showed me some of the letters from a small pile on his desk. 'Dear Joe,' and 'Dear Lieutenant Leonard,' the notes read, 'I'm sorry I took part in the strike ...' 'You'll get no letter from me, Joe,' I said to him.

Now and then over the next few weeks either Joe Leonard or an orderly NCO would remind me that I still hadn't written my letter of apology, but eventually the matter dropped. Many months later, however, when the strike was all but forgotten, Joe Leonard reminded me about the letter. 'You were the only one who didn't write an apology,' he said, grinning. 'As a matter of fact,' he went on, 'there was a bet among the officers as to whether or not you'd apologise. I knew you'd never write it, Seán,' he said, 'I had to admire the way you held out.'

Kilkenny barracks had been constructed in the traditional style of British barracks, with a cubicle at the entrance of each long barrack room to provide a small sleeping compartment for the NCO in charge of the barrack room. Early one morning, after an uneventful night of guard duty, it was my turn to begin reveille by waking up the NCOs in each of the barrack rooms. One of the NCOs, Jackie Foy, had turned in very late that night and I thought I'd have some fun waking him up. I knew Jackie quite well; he'd been a good IRA man during the Black and Tan War and was now a sergeant in the National Army.

'Come on! Wake up! Wake up!' I shouted when I entered his room. 'Show a leg there! Time to get up!'

'Leave me alone,' he growled from beneath his blankets. 'I'll shoot you if you don't get out of here,' and he reached towards his pillow. I made a fast grab for his pillow and beating him to it, pulled out a .45 Webley.

'Now,' I said, 'who's going to shoot who?' I walked up to the foot of his bed while Jackie rubbed the sleep from his eyes and sat up. 'Get out of that bed,' I grinned at him, 'or I'll blow you out.'

'Be careful, Seán,' he said, 'it's loaded.'

'Oh, that's different,' I said, and quickly lowered the revolver. Then Jackie said the revolver *wasn't* loaded. Just to make sure, I raised the revolver again and glanced down the barrel. As a rule, one can see the nose of a bullet if there's one in the barrel. I didn't see one there, but I put the revolver on half cock in order to turn and check each cylinder. After five 'clicks' I agreed that the revolver was empty. 'What's the use of having a revolver under your pillow if it's not loaded?' I asked him.

'No need to,' he said.

'Now I *will* shoot,' I said, pointing the revolver just above his head, 'so you'd better get out anyway.' I pulled the trigger, and in the instant roar a piece of wood tore out of the wall above his head.

Jackie went as white as a sheet. I tossed him the gun and he slapped it under his pillow, while I dashed out of the room. The sound of the shot woke everyone up and they were asking, 'What was that? Who's been shot?' I never let on, and neither did Jackie. Later the two of us examined the hole in the wall where the bullet was lodged, and agreed it was only by the grace of God that I missed him.

The sound of that shot I accidentally fired at Jackie Foy was probably the first shot heard in Kilkenny since our arrival there, but we hadn't been in Kilkenny barracks very long before we became aware that an anti-Treatyite element existed in the town. We heard ugly rumours of an impending civil war between those who repudiated the Anglo-Irish Treaty and those who were prepared to abide by it.

Hardly anyone in Ireland – especially those who'd participated in the War of Independence – was happy with the terms of the Treaty, but since it had been accepted by the Irish delegation sent to negotiate a treaty with England and their acceptance subsequently ratified by Dáil Éireann, the consensus of Irish opinion agreed to honour the Treaty. Although the terms of the Treaty were unjust to a nation that had paid such a terrible price to secure some of its independence, and were accepted only under the threat of dire retribution for its rejection, we of the National Army accepted the arguments of Michael Collins and Arthur Griffith that the terms were the best that Ireland could obtain at that time. While it became increasingly apparent that Lloyd George and the British delegation had negotiated treacherously and were guilty of the worst sort of duplicity, we knew that the Irish delegation had negotiated in good faith, and that Ireland's honour should remain unsullied. For us to repudiate a treaty we had already accepted would have debased the reputation of our newly independent state and branded us for being as perfidious as the British.

The seriousness of the crisis towards which Ireland was headed came to us one morning just as dawn was breaking when I woke up to find Captain Paddy Daly in the centre of our barrack room quietly but firmly rousing everyone from his sleep. He told us to get dressed quickly, cautioning us to make as little noise as possible, and to get our rifles and bandoliers of ammunition.

He explained that it had just been discovered that the Wexford flying column had disappeared from their quarters – taking their rifles and ammo with them – and that the guard room was deserted and the rear gates left wide open. When he gave the order, we all rushed out – some of the lads still barefooted – and made a dash for the rear gates which we immediately closed and secured. Leaving a couple of lads to guard the gates, some of us climbed the barracks' walls to man the abandoned sentry positions while the rest made a thorough search of the guard room and the barrack rooms allocated to the Wexford flying column.

The search party discovered only one remaining member of the flying column: a useless alcoholic bound and tied to his bed. Not wanting to be encumbered by him, his comrades had left him behind. Paddy Daly closely questioned the poor fellow, but the man was still inebriated and could remember nothing about his comrades' action or where they had gone.

Lieutenant Joe Leonard and a few officers then boarded a Crossley tender and, telling us that they didn't intend to make prisoners of the Wexford column who'd deserted the barracks but only wished to retrieve their arms and ammunition, they drove off to scour the countryside for twenty miles around Kilkenny. Unfortunately, they found no trace of the fleeing men and returned empty-handed.

Because of the mounting crisis over the Treaty, and aware of the agonising dilemma facing us as we considered the likelihood of being ordered to fire upon former comrades if a civil war erupted, Captain Daly assembled our two companies on the barracks' square to listen carefully to what he had to say.

In a calm, deliberate manner Paddy Daly reviewed the issues at stake, outlining objectively the respective positions being adopted by those for the Treaty and those against the Treaty. Then, after a pause, he told us we each had to decide – once and for all – where we stood on the Treaty, asking us to consider carefully the choice we each must make. He appealed for any man who could not in conscience support the Treaty to step out and leave the National Army. He assured us that no animosity would be shown against anyone who stepped forward; that every facility would be given to enable those who wished to return to Dublin, to do so. He also promised that no action would subsequently be taken against those who left the army and returned to Dublin. All he asked for, he said, was that those who wished to leave should hand in to stores their uniforms, rifles, ammunition, and their other military gear before they left.

Not a single man stepped out.

In fact, to the best of my recollection, only one man ever deserted the Dublin Guards either before or during the Civil War. I knew him well. His name is immaterial now, but he was a popular, red-haired fellow who'd once belonged to the Active Service Unit. During the Civil War he went over to the anti-Treatyites and became one of their best fighters until the Free State detectives caught up with him. As a result of the brutal beating some of that murderous gang gave him, he died 'prematurely.'

As we stood on the square of Kilkenny barracks listening to the words of Captain Daly, I'm sure my comrades felt as I did, that our commitment to Michael Collins had been made even before we transferred as Volunteers from the IRA to the National Army, and that our loyalty remained unshakeable. Collins – together with most of the IRA Headquarters staff – supported the Treaty, and those like myself who considered Collins to still be our leader were prepared to follow him in whatever course he decided to take. Such was our faith in Mick Collins. It was as simple as that.

I believed Collins when he spoke of the Treaty as being at least a stepping-stone to the Republic we all eventually wanted, and that the Treaty gave us freedom – 'not the ultimate freedom (as he put it) that all nations desire and develop to, but the freedom to achieve it.' I shared, too, in his vision of an end to England's economic and cultural 'penetration' of Ireland, and in his conviction that the Treaty gave us as a nation the opportunity to stand on our own feet. As Arthur Griffith had pointed out in the Dáil when he proposed the formal ratification of the Treaty, Ireland had – for the first time in over seven hundred years – treated with England on equal terms and had secured the right to her own army. I was convinced, as Seán MacEoin was when he seconded Griffith's motion, that with the removal of the British army, the Irish people could – with its own army to defend them – 'develop our own nation in our own way.'

As he dismissed us, Captain Paddy Daly warned us to henceforth keep a careful watch on our rifles and ammunition, and to be particularly alert when on guard duty. From then on, we carried our rifles – loaded – everywhere we went. We even took them to church with us when we went to mass, although Paddy Daly remarked with bitter regret that he never thought he'd see the day when Irish troops would need to carry loaded rifles with them when they attended a church parade in their own country.

Undoubtedly there were anti-Treatyites in Kilkenny town, but contrary to reports that they had two 'barracks' – one in John Street and another in Parliament Street – I can recall only one overt indication of their presence; they were ensconced in a large, two-storeyed private dwelling located incongruously among a row of shops in a street that ran parallel to the River Nore. The house was distinguished from its neighbours by having a small garden in its front instead of a projecting shop window. The parlour window facing the street was kept wide open and passers-by could plainly see a Lewis gun mounted on a table behind the windowsill, with a couple of anti-Treatyites sitting on a table beside the gun. Although their pose was distinctly provocative, we of the National Army took no action against them until one day their snipers started firing at us. We had tolerated their taunts as we passed by their 'garrison' – and even endured the embarrassment of having onlookers (especially the girls) snicker at our lack of retaliation – but the day the anti-Treatyites took a few pot shots at us we quickly struck back.

Orders were given that the outpost be seized and a small party of us approached the house – with our rifles at the ready – by advancing along both sides of the shopping street. We expected the anti-Treatyites to open fire on us, but finding no opposition to our approach we decided to rush the building when we were close enough to make a dash for the front door. Three of us raced for the front steps unchallenged and, when we tried the door, found it opened readily when we turned the door knob. Rushing through the hallway to the rear of the house – followed by the rest of our party who began a

Neill Kerr, Sr.

Tom Kerr.

Stephen Lanigan (left) and Tom Kerr (right) during internment at Ballykinlar Camp.

Volunteers John Pinkman (left) and Bernie Meehan (right) before their arrest at Hall Road.

Members of the Liverpool Company, IRA, released from Dartmoor Prison, 14 February 1922. Bernie Meehan (standing, far left), Paddy Lowe (seated, second from left), John Pinkman (seated, far right).

The Findlater Building facing Sackville Street (now O'Connell Street). (Photo: Ian Finlay.)

The curtained window (first floor, far right) in the Findlater Building from which the bullet that mortally wounded Cathal Brugha was fired. (Photo: Ian Finlay.)

View of Thomas' Lane from the window in the Findlater Building from which the bullet that mortally wounded Cathal Brugha was fired. (Photo: Ian Finlay.)

Tom Flood, Commandant of the Dublin Guards' Flying Column.

John A. Pinkman, 'A' Company, Dublin Guards, National Army, Kilkenny barracks.

Some of the members of Commdt Tom Flood's Flying Column in Mallow. John Pinkman is seated, second from the left.

thorough search of all the rooms – we found that the anti-Treatyites had fled before us. When we reached the garden wall behind the house we could see the bold 'garrison' running wildly across a field towards a bridge over the Nore – without a single shot being fired during the whole affair!

After that confrontation, Kilkenny became once again a pleasant, peaceful country town whose only sounds were those of commerce, horse-drawn carts, church bells, and the cawing of crows. In the barracks we resumed the normal routine of garrison troops concentrating on perfecting our drill and learning the skills of soldiering, while at the same time keeping alert for anti-Treatyite hostilities. The crisis over the Treaty was still unresolved and attempts in Dublin to reach a compromise between the pro-Treaty and the anti-Treaty leaders had failed. On the national scene, the political situation was grimmer than ever, but in Kilkenny there was little reflection on the events in Dublin. Absent, too, were the taunts that once annoyed us.

Officially – and properly – we were troops of the National Army, although we were often referred to as the Free State troops or, less kindly, the 'Staters'; those who hated us called us the 'Green and Tans'. Anti-Treatyites who actively opposed the Provisional Government of the Irish Free State – and the National Army – styled themselves 'Republicans'. Following the ratification of the Treaty by Dáil Éireann on 7 January 1922, those senior officers of the IRA Executive grandiloquently proclaimed themselves and their followers as the 'Executive Forces'. We knew them as 'Irregulars,' but when we saw for ourselves their inept tactics as 'soldiers' and their dishonourable behaviour as Irishmen we contemptuously called them Paddy-Joes or, more colloquially, 'padjoes' – a derogatory term equivalent to the English epithet 'yokels' or 'bumpkins.' It must be borne in mind, however, that most of our lads were Dubliners and retained the Dubliners' traditional disdain for Irish country people.

Despite the crisis fomenting in Dublin, we resumed our garrison duties in Kilkenny barracks. The pace of our soldiering became steadier as we acquired more confidence in our military skills and I was just beginning to find the routine tedious when an officer named

Allman came up to me in the barracks one day and announced he was going to form a corps of mechanical engineers for the army. Allman was a Kerryman who had emigrated to America where he'd worked as a professional engineer in San Francisco. While in the States he'd played a prominent part in Clan na Gael and, together with a fellow by the name of Fitzgerald, was said to have been responsible for smuggling the first Thompson submachine guns into Ireland. Allman had learned that I'd been an apprenticed fitter in Liverpool and he asked me to join the Mechanical Engineering Corps which he was starting.

I was very enthusiastic about the formation of a corps of mechanical engineers, and he took me over to the ordnance section where he gave me a bunch of keys for the workshop and store-room. 'I'm going to put you in charge,' Allman said. 'I'll find you another man and then we'll make you a sergeant.' And that was how the Mechanical Engineering Corps of the National Army began!

For the next week or so I had nothing to do but eat my meals and sit in an ordnance store-room looking out the windows. Allman had not been able to find the mechanic he was looking for, and without a tap of work to do I soon found myself becoming terribly bored. I missed the companionship of the rest of the lads who were parading and drilling, and wondered if I'd made the right decision when I threw in my lot with Allman.

Then one morning at breakfast we heard that there was going to be some trouble in the town and the lads were ordered to 'fall in' and prepare for an attack. Apparently a force of Irregulars had quietly infiltrated Kilkenny and seized Ormonde castle and the tower adjacent to St Canice's Anglican cathedral. We were warned to keep off the barracks' square because the tower overlooked the square and there was a chance that Irregular snipers in the tower might shoot us; we were, in fact, confined to barracks for the remainder of that day. I remember watching Commandant Prout mounting a rifle on a tripod in a corner of the square and sitting on a chair behind the tripod taking pot shots at the tower – for all the world like a sporting gentleman seated on his shooting stick blasting away at wild fowl.

The next day as I saw my old company preparing for action – checking their rifles and loading up with ammunition prior to heading out to attack the Irregulars – I locked up the ordnance section, grabbed my rifle and ammo, and fell in with the rest of the boys. Joe Leonard spotted me in the ranks and asked me why I was there. 'I've nothing else to do,' I said. 'I'm tired of sitting around in the ordnance stores ...'

Joe laughed and shook his head. 'You might as well join in then,' he said.

Our company marched out of the barracks and down the road towards St Canice's tower. Flushing the Irregulars out of the tower proved difficult because the snipers in the tower were well positioned to pick us off as we approached. They kept up a steady hail of accurate fire but we eventually rushed the tower capturing most of its defenders.

We hoped that the Irregulars had been taught a sharp lesson when we demonstrated how readily we rid St Canice's tower of them, but those who'd managed to avoid being captured joined up with their comrades in Ormonde castle, and because of their continual belligerency we had little choice the following day but to attack the castle, too. When we reached a low stone wall facing the castle on the far side of the River Nore, we spread out along the wall and crouching down behind the thick stones opened fire on the Irregulars. It was the first time that I'd ever fired a service rifle in action and during the excitement the recoil of my .303 Lee-Enfield nearly tore off my shoulder!

After we had exchanged a few inconclusive volleys with the Irregulars in the castle, some of us were detailed to return to the town with orders to clear a party of anti-Treatyites from a house in which they'd established an outpost. Splitting into two sections, we rushed the house from opposite ends of the street but the anti-Treatyites abandoned their outpost without firing a shot as they saw us approach, and we then returned to the attack on the castle. By that time the main body of our company had reached the castle gates which were firmly closed against us. There seemed to be no other way in which we could seize the castle than through its main gates and I recall us crouching beneath the castle walls wondering aloud how we could force our way in. Then one of our boys (whose name, I believe, was Hudson) went off to get a lorry and on his return drove the lorry straight into the castle gates smashing them open. The rest of us, who'd been crouching against the castle walls on either side of the gates, charged into the castle courtyard as soon as the gates had been breached and, fanning out in the courtyard, we met some of the Irregulars coming forward to surrender.

While we were gathering up those Irregulars who'd promptly capitulated, we noticed several of their comrades trying to escape from the castle and a few of us dashed forward to pursue and capture them. I caught up with one of them and confiscated a .455-calibre Mark V Webley revolver he was carrying in a leather holster but in the general confusion the fellow managed to slip away from me. He was a young fellow of about my own age and I was contented enough with getting his revolver.

After we had gained control of Ormonde castle, Joe Leonard detailed a squad to guard it and I was immediately put on sentry duty at its battered main entrance. Many of the Kilkenny townspeople came to take a look at the castle when all the shooting was over, and I found myself the object of considerable attention as I paced up and down with my rifle. A news photographer took my picture and a few days later there I was – with my rifle – on the front page of *The Kilkenny People!* The lads in our company teased me about the photograph, but I was as proud as punch and bought a couple of copies of the newspaper which I sent home to my mother.

The Irregulars that we'd captured at the castle were marched off to Kilkenny barracks where they were held as prisoners – along with the rest of the anti-Treatyites we'd rounded up in Kilkenny – for a few days. Nothing very drastic happened to them; after a scolding they were released and sent home!

Significant as they may have been at the time (during the first week of May, 1922), our brief clashes with the anti-Treatyite Irregulars in Kilkenny town have been greatly exaggerated by many authors of second-hand accounts published in recent years. Calton Younger, an Australian who has written a generally fair and mainly accurate account of the Civil War, makes the encounter in Kilkenny seem like Fort Sumter![43] The claim made by Eoin Neeson that 'anti-Treaty forces tried to drive pro-Treaty troops out of strategic Kilkenny City'[44] is simply incorrect. In fact, those anti-Treatyites in Kilkenny who showed any belligerency did so as mere tokenism and were quickly rounded up and then sent home. Nor can I remember any agreement 'which left positions to both sides in the city.'[45] The anti-Treatyites were left with *no* positions in Kilkenny!

But the funniest story that I've read concerning the Kilkenny showdown is the one that tells of Tom Flood and Joe Leonard rushing down from Beggar's Bush barracks – with two hundred men of the Dublin Guards aboard a special train[46] – to join in the fray ... like a scene from a Hollywood movie where the federales come roaring into some Mexican town. Hell! 'A' and 'B' Companies of the Dublin Guards were in Kilkenny long before the confrontation began. Joe Leonard was there all the time. I should know ... because he was a lieutenant in our company and I was under his direct command the day hostilities began.

To prevent the padjoes returning and re-establishing themselves in St Canice's tower, we mounted a guard within the tower itself and in the surrounding graveyard. A Protestant cleric and his wife who lived close to St Canice's cathedral sent us over a big supper of sandwiches, tea and cake on our first night there and that first night's guard duty was unforgettable. The sentries crouching among the headstones were more afraid of ghosts than they were of the padjoes! Some young fellows came into the tower swearing they'd seen corpses climbing out of their graves, and the relieving sentries were afraid to go out, especially after a couple of shots were fired in the dark by nervous guards. The sergeant in charge of us finally solved the problem by calling everyone inside and bolting the door. He left one lad to guard the door and then told us to stretch ourselves out on the floor and get some sleep!

A few days after our confrontation with the anti-Treatyites, and when Kilkenny town had quietened down again, Allman asked me to rejoin the corps of mechanical engineers he was so determined to get started. But I refused to join him because I knew I'd be far happier if I remained with my company. Allman eventually found his mechanic, big Seán Keating, and made him a sergeant. Seán and I were very good friends. He'd belonged to the Active Service Unit and had taken part in the Bloody Sunday job. When he left the army, Seán joined the Garda Síochána and was stationed in Dublin where I often met him on patrol duty.

One of my happiest memories of Kilkenny was the luxurious bedroom I was given high up in Ormonde castle when I was assigned to guard duty in the castle. The bedroom window overlooked the Nore and the lovely countryside beyond the river, and I spent many a pleasant hour quietly contemplating the beauty and serenity surrounding Kilkenny as peace settled over the area once again.

My sojourn in Ormonde castle ended when I was told to report back to Kilkenny barracks and rejoin my company which had been ordered to return to our headquarters at Beggar's Bush barracks, Dublin, where Mick Collins – our Commander-in-Chief – had established his General Headquarters. The day following our arrival at Beggar's Bush barracks we were assembled in columns-of-route – with our rifles – and told we were going to take over Portobello barracks, one of the last barracks still remaining under British army control.

As we marched down Rathmines Road towards Portobello barracks we noticed that the British had cut down the flag pole just as they had done so at Kilkenny barracks, but before we entered the gates we halted while a couple of our lads ran to a building contractor's yard beside the barracks in order to get a ladder. The two lads returned with a good, long ladder and someone tied the Irish tricolour to the top of the ladder before they placed the ladder at the gate in such a manner that the Irish flag hung right over the gate. Then we marched in.

Within Portobello barracks the British Tommies were lined up very smartly on the parade square waiting for our arrival. I can imagine that they expected to see an awkward lot of half-trained country gobshites shuffle in, and I'm sure we disappointed them. We had drilled to perfection in Kilkenny just for this sort of occasion. Upon our column halting in the parade square, the squad previously selected to mount the new guard immediately swung into the drill of taking over – one by one – from the old guard; the British Tommies, relieved of their duty, returning to join the rest of the British troops.

There was a 'general salute', the old guard dismissed, and then the contingent of British troops marched out through the barracks gates – right under the tricolour. We were then dismissed and moved into the barracks. It was as simple and as orderly as that, but for all of us it was a very proud experience.

7

MOST OF THE LADS IN our company were Dubliners and once we were settled down in Portobello barracks they were able to go and visit their relatives and friends in the city. But my family hadn't seen me since I left Liverpool shortly after my release from Dartmoor Prison. I knew how worried they must have been, especially since they knew I was in Kilkenny during the fighting there, so I asked Joe Leonard if I could have a few days to go across to Liverpool. Joe said certainly I could go and gave me a chit granting me ten days leave. I was delighted at the prospect of a holiday at home and told him I'd be crossing to Holyhead on the mail boat that day.

I was so excited that afternoon that I went down to tell the Lowes the good news that I was going home on leave. Jimmy Lowe – Paddy's brother – offered to see me off at Westland Row Station where I was to catch the train for Dun Laoghaire, but because I had to return to Portobello barracks to pack my gear, he promised to meet me at the station.

When I arrived at the station, Jimmy Lowe wasn't there and having waited on the platform as long as I could I finally climbed aboard the train just before it was ready to pull out. But I had no sooner made myself comfortable in an empty compartment than I looked up to find Jimmy Lowe and Hughie Early panting heavily and knocking on the windows. I was surpised to find Hughie Early on the platform, because I knew that he'd joined the anti-Treatyites, and I'd never liked him anyway. Jimmy Lowe and I exchanged a few words but then Hughie Early butted in.

'Are you going to Liverpool?' he asked. 'Aren't you afraid to be going over there?'

'Oh, no,' I said. 'I'm not worried. There's peace now ... at least I hope so!'

'I'd be worried if I went over,' he said.

I told him that the Tans wouldn't bother me; those of them who hadn't found jobs would be perfectly happy to do nothing but collect the dole. 'In any case,' I said, 'I don't think there were any Tans from Bootle.'

Just then the guard blew his whistle and the engine blasted off some steam as the train prepared to depart. 'And you're not worried?' Hughie Early asked. 'If I were you, I *would* be worried!'

'I can take care of myself,' I said sharply, suddenly getting annoyed with his persistent and unexpected concern for my safety.

'Oh, you can, can you?' he said sarcastically.

'You're damned right I can,' I said, putting my hand into an inside pocket of my coat and showing him the butt of the .455 Webley I'd taken from the Irregular in Kilkenny.

The train gave a lurch and slowly started to pull out from Westland Row Station.

'Goodbye, Jimmy,' I shouted. 'Goodbye!'

On the boat to Holyhead I found myself reconsidering Hughie Early's warning, but the more I thought about it, the more satisfied I was that I'd nothing to worry about from the Black and Tans or the Orangemen in Liverpool.

After the short sea trip from Dun Laoghaire to Holyhead, I caught the train to Liverpool, and as I was walking through one of the carriages I met Neill Kerr and his wife who had also travelled over from Dublin. Neill was still one of Mick Collins' most trusted agents in England and often travelled back and forth between Dublin and Liverpool. Neill was very happy to see me and both he and his wife made me promise I'd visit them at their home in Florida Street while I was in Liverpool.

While I was home I met many of my old pals whom I hadn't seen since the night of the farm fires; the news quickly got around that I was home again and some of the boys came around to our house and we had great times together. Then one evening I went to see a particular friend of mine, Frank Hennessy, who lived on the other side of Liverpool. Frank worked in a stockbroker's office but he was very interested in politics and he and I used to attend meetings of the Independent Labour Party before I was arrested.

When I returned home that night about half-past ten or eleven o'clock, Tommy O'Malley, an ex-volunteer of the Liverpool Company of the IRA, was waiting for me outside the front door of our house. I hadn't seen him since before the Hall Road job and invited him to come in and have some supper with me, but he refused to come in saying he just wanted to talk to me. I told him how upset my mother would be if she knew he was on the doorstep and would not come in for at least a drop of tea, because his family came from the West of Ireland and my parents knew them very well. We chatted for a while but it was getting late and I warned him that he might miss the last tramcar back into Liverpool.

I was just about to bid him good night when he gave a sudden wave of his hand and three other fellows emerged out of the darkness and ran towards us; one came directly across from the other side of Rimrose Road, another from the left towards Cranworth Street, and the third from the direction of Grove Street on the right. I couldn't have been more surprised when the three strangers ran up to surround me on a signal from the fellow to whom I'd been so innocently chatting.

'I want that gun,' said my ex-comrade who then dropped all pretences of cordiality.

'What gun?' I asked. 'What are you talking about?'

'You have a gun, haven't you?' he asked.

'Me?' I said. 'Are you out of your mind? Me, carry a gun, after getting five years in Dartmoor? I wouldn't dream of carrying a gun!'

'I've got orders to shoot you if you don't hand over that gun,' he said. 'I'll drop you in the sewer if you don't give us that gun.'

'Well,' I said, 'I suppose you'll have to shoot me and I can't do anything about it because I've got no gun. If you want to, you can search the house.'

One of them knocked on the door and when my mother opened it, we all trooped in. My sisters heard the commotion of our entrance and came rushing out of the kitchen to see the unexpected 'guests,' but as I tried to explain the arrival of the four fellows one of them pulled out his revolver and announced they were going to search the house. Another one of them saw me edging my way along the wall towards the staircase and he, too, pulled out a revolver threatening to shoot me if I moved any further. Then my mother recognised one of the gang as the son of one of her best friends from the West of Ireland and told him he was a shame and a disgrace to his family.

We all went into the kitchen where a big coal fire was roaring in the grate and one of the gunmen started to give a speech about the Treaty and the Free State. I began to laugh at him and told my mother and my sisters not to pay any attention to him because he didn't know what he was talking about. 'If you're going to search the house,' I said, 'get on with it and don't be giving us one of Dev's auld speeches.' He became very angry and said he'd shoot me if I interfered with their search for the gun. While he'd been talking, Annie, my youngest sister, had slipped out of the kitchen and into the back yard, but one of the gang caught her and forced her at gun point to return to the kitchen. She was crying when they came in.

The men searched the kitchen for the revolver but couldn't find it, and were about to go upstairs when my mother asked me – in front of the searchers – if I had the gun they were looking for. I told her I knew how upset she'd be if I ever brought a gun into the house, but one of the gang said he knew I had a gun; that I'd had a gun when I left Dublin and that he'd been given orders in Dublin to get the gun off me.

'All right,' I said. 'I did have a gun when I left Dublin, but I don't have it now.'

'Well, where is it?' they asked.

'I gave it to Neill Kerr. I met him on the train from Holyhead and when I told him I was carrying a gun, he made me hand it over. He said I was a fool to have a gun on me and that it would only get me into trouble. He said he'd send it back to Dublin for me and I could get it when I returned after my leave. It must be in Ireland by now.'

'We'll see,' they said, and told me they were going to take me to Neill Kerr who lived in Florida Street, about a mile from our house.

It was a bright, moonlit night and I thought I'd be able to give them the slip because I knew the streets between Rimrose Road and

Florida Street like the back of my hand. But they warned me not to try to make a break for it, and with their hands in their coat pockets two of them walked right behind me while the other two walked one on each side of me. There was scarcely a soul abroad in the streets but when we reached the fire station on Strand Road I tried to confuse and distract my escort by telling them that we were about to pass a police station. My ruse didn't work and the fellow on my left jabbed me with the barrel of his revolver which he held in his pocket.

Eventually we reached Florida Street and when we knocked on the door of Neill Kerr's house, Neill let us in. As surprised as he was to see us call on him at such a late hour of the night, Neill began to welcome us to his house until I quickly interrupted him.

'Wait a minute, Neill,' I said. 'Do you remember that gun I gave you on the train from Holyhead. Well, these fellows were sent over from Dublin with orders to shoot me if I didn't give them the gun. I told them that you took it from me in case I got myself in trouble with it, and that you were going to send it back to Dublin.'

'That's right, Seán,' he said, without as much as batting an eyelid. 'The gun's over in Dublin now. I did it for your own good. You were a bloody fool to try and bring it over here. The Tan War is over and we want no more trouble.'

I told Neill that the fellows looking for the gun had threatened to shoot me in front of my mother unless they got the revolver, and that they'd even searched our house in Rimrose Road. The poor fools who'd come looking for the gun didn't really know what to do next so they began to curse me for supporting the Treaty and being a 'Stater', saying I was, among other things, a 'Green and Tan'.

Then they turned to Neill Kerr, one of the greatest Irishmen I've ever met. In 1916, Neill and his three sons – Tom, Jack and Neill – gave up everything they had in Liverpool in order to go over to Dublin for the Rising.[47] After his release from internment, he became one of Mick Collins' most trusted agents in England during the Tan War. He not only organised the smuggling of arms to Ireland, but he met De Valera in Liverpool after Dev's escape from Lincoln Prison in February 1919 and hid him in the home of Mrs Dan MacCarthy. It was Neill Kerr who arranged for Harry Boland to be smuggled to the US aboard the *Celtic*, and later on, in June 1919 he got out of his sick bed in Dublin to go across to Liverpool and arrange for De Valera to be smuggled to the US. Later in the same year on Saturday 25 October he was one of the small party that helped the six IRA prisoners (including Austen Stack and Piaras Béaslaí) escape from Manchester Jail. Yet those four anti-Treayite gunmen told Neill he was a traitor to Ireland and that along with Collins he had sold out Ireland to the British. I tried to interrupt the stream of insults and abuse they threw at Neill, but one of them pushed me onto a sofa, and, telling me to shut up, held the muzzle of his revolver against my head.

Neill was standing with his back to the fireplace. He waited until they ended their tirade of curses and insults and then tore open his loose-necked shirt.

'I'm a traitor, am I?' he said calmly. 'Well, if I ever betrayed Ireland then I deserve to be shot. Shoot me now, if I'm a traitor.'

One of the bastards was actually levelling his revolver at Neill's chest when Mrs Kerr came rushing into the front parlour from the kitchen.

'Oh my God!' she screamed. 'Is this what they're going to do to you, Neill?' And then she collapsed in a faint on the floor.

'Look what you've done to my wife!' roared Neill. 'I'll kill you!' He lunged for the gunman, who turned and fled for the door with Neill charging after him. Then the fellow who'd been holding his revolver against my head panicked and he, too, dashed for the door, quickly followed by the last two members of the search party.

The dark, narrow hallway outside the parlour became a scene of frantic confusion as the gunmen scrambled to reach the front door and unlock it. Neill cornered one of the gunmen against the wall and was hammering away at him with his big fists, while I tangled with another. The fight ended only when somebody finally managed to get the front door open and the gunmen began tumbling out of the house. The last one to leave was literally kicked out of the house when my boot drove into his backside.

Neill locked the door after them and we returned to the front parlour where we found Mrs Kerr sitting by the fireside. A quickwitted woman, she'd merely pretended to faint in order to throw the intruders off guard.

'Where's the gun?' Neill asked me when he'd caught his breath.

'It's safely hidden at home,' I said. 'I wasn't going to let those padjoes get it.'

'Jasus! Jasus!' he said and shook his head. Then he told me I should stay at his house for the rest of the night in case the fellows looking for the gun might be lying in wait for me outside. But I told him I wanted to get home again as soon as possible, because when I left our house in Rimrose Road my mother was crying and my sisters were on their knees saying the rosary.

Neill made me wait for another fifteen or twenty minutes while he kept close watch through the curtains to see if any of the gang was hanging around in the street. Before I left, Neill told me to walk in the middle of the road and keep my eyes open. 'God be with you, Seán,' he said, as I slipped out of the front door. I walked down Florida Street and zig-zagged my way through the streets and back alleys between Stanley Road and Rimrose Road. There was nobody in the streets and I reached home without having seen or heard anything of the men who'd been so desperate to get my revolver. When I knocked on the door, my sister Annie opened it, and when she saw I was safely back again she threw her arms around me and showered me with kisses.

The rest of the family were so relieved to see me that they knelt down and said another decade of the rosary before I told them about what happened at Neill Kerr's. I warned them that if anyone came knocking on the door they weren't to open it; they were to awaken me and *I* would answer the door.

My mother took me aside and asked me about the gun and what I'd done with it.

'It's upstairs,' I said. 'It's in a wooden box under my bed.'

'Oh Mother of God!' she said. 'You've had the gun all the time!

'Yes,' I said, 'and if they ever come around here again I'll shoot them.'

I slept late that morning, so it was almost noon before I got up and discovered that the revolver was missing from the box beneath my bed. When I went downstairs I asked the rest of the family what had happened to my gun, but they wouldn't say a word; they merely smiled knowingly and winked at each other. Finally my mother said that Neill Kerr had called about eight o'clock to see whether or not I'd got home safely, and then he promised to send a man about an hour later to pick up the revolver and take it across to Ireland.

That afternoon I went to see Neill who told me that he'd sent the revolver over to Dublin with one of his trusted men. 'Mick Collins will have it now,' he said, 'and you'll have to get it from him,' and we both laughed.

When my leave was over and I returned to Dublin, I went straight to the Lowes and told Jimmy about the attempt to get my revolver in Liverpool. I asked him bluntly if he had told Hughie Early that I was going over to Liverpool on leave, but Jimmy denied having done so. I found it hard to believe it was merely a coincidence that Early happened to be on the platform when Jimmy came to see me off. But Jimmy Lowe told me that immediately after the train had departed from Westland Row Station, Hughie Early hired a hackney cab and drove to Nelson's Pillar in Sackville Street where he rounded up three or four anti-Treatyites who then took a taxi to Dun Laoghiare in an attempt to stop me before the mail boat left. By the time the taxi reached Dun Laoghaire, however, the boat had just left the harbour.

Jimmy went on to tell me that Martin – one of the Four Courts crowd – had vowed to shoot me on sight if ever I showed up in Dublin again, and that although they didn't get the revolver they were determined to get me.

I reported the whole affair to Joe Leonard when I got back to Portobello barracks. Joe didn't say very much but he let me understand that I was free to take whatever action I wanted against Martin and his cronies.

That afternoon I decided to call Martin's bluff and give him and his gang the opportunity to carry out their threats. Having first made a couple of 'preliminary arrangements' and taking along a little 'protection', I took a tramcar to Sackville Street and got off at the General Post Office. I walked across to the pillar, and then I crossed over to North Earl Street, a well-known haunt of the Four Courts crowd, and took my time as I walked towards Gardiner Street. I had often seen Martin in his black hat and trench coat skulking in the doorways along North Earl Street and hoped to find him there. I must admit that I had a terrible feeling that I would be shot in the back before I had the opportunity of drawing my own gun, but if I saw anyone pulling out a revolver I was determined to shoot it out with him. Fortunately, my stroll along North Earl Street passed without incident and I returned to Portobello barracks unharmed. After that, neither Martin nor his erstwhile assassins ever bothered me again.

8

ON SUNDAY 25 JUNE OUR company was sent on a route march from Portobello barracks to Bodenstown (where Wolfe Tone lies buried) and back again. The purpose of the march – with rifles and bandoliers of ammunition – was to provide a 'show of strength,' but very few of us had much strength left by the time we returned to our barracks. I went to bed right away because my ankles were swollen and I felt I was coming down with a cold.

Since no activities had been planned for the company the following day (Monday 26 June), I spent most of the day in bed, but I was awakened in the evening and told to join a party being sent to guard Mountjoy Prison – or the 'Joy,' as it's generally known in Dublin.

Earlier that day, Leo Henderson had led a group of anti-Treatyites garrisoned in the Four Courts and raided Ferguson's garage in Lower Baggot Street – where Massey-Ferguson now has a showroom. Henderson's group commandeered all the vehicles in the garage claiming they needed them for the fight against the British in the north. But Michael Collins couldn't allow this and sent a party of troops to grab Henderson and put him in Mountjoy Prison.

We were sent to guard the 'Joy' in case any of the anti-Treatyites attacked it in an attempt to free Henderson, but after a couple of spells of guard duty I became so ill with the feverish cold I'd caught during the march to Bodenstown that I was sent back to Portobello barracks first thing on Wednesday morning, 28 June, and told to report sick. When I arrived there, the doctor took one look at me and having prescribed a tonic ordered me into the sick bay for immediate rest. It wasn't until Wednesday afternoon – when I awoke after a fitful sleep – that I learned that in retaliation for our capture of Leo Henderson, the Four Courts crowd had kidnapped General 'Ginger' O'Connell, Deputy Chief-of-Staff of the National Army, and that this was the last straw for Mick Collins and the Provisional Government who'd demanded the Four Courts garrison to surrender by 4.00am.

Nearly half an hour after the deadline one of the field guns lobbed a shell at the Four Courts building.

The news that the Four Courts had been shelled intermittently during the day aroused interest but no excitement among the lads in the sick bay. It was generally believed that the besieged garrison – many of whom had never been exposed to an armed attack of any sort – would be overawed by the firing of the field guns and the knowledge that they were hemmed in by armed and experienced troops of the National Army, and the affair would be all over within a matter of hours, probably before the next morning.

However, shortly after dawn the next morning (Thursday 29 June), I was awakened by the excitement in the sick bay as somebody was announcing the news that Portobello barracks was practically deserted and that an all-out assault had been launched on the Four Courts by the Dublin Guards. Apparently the previous day's shelling had little effect, after all, on the anti-Treatyite garrison. The eighteen-pound shells fired at the massive walls of the Four Courts were only shrapnel shells, not high-explosive shells, and to make matters worse the relatively inexperienced gunners were hopelessly inaccurate. I've often speculated since that a couple – just two – twenty-five-pound high-explosive shells accurately placed might have prevented all the subsequent fighting of the Civil War.

As I lay there in the sick bay that morning regretting that I was confined to bed while the rest of my company was out fighting, I heard a lorry come roaring into the barracks and stop outside the sick bay. When I took a look through the window beside my bed to see what the commotion was, I saw a badly wounded soldier covered with blood being brought in from a lorry not much bigger than a modern milk van but with high wooden sides. Then a nurse dashed into the ward looking for an empty bed but there weren't any.

'Give him mine,' I said, and I got out of bed, put on my uniform and went outside to talk to the driver. He told me that the fighting at the Four Courts was worse than had been expected and he and his mate had been sent back to the barracks to pick up a load of ammunition. He said he needed someone to help him load the boxes of ammo and ride in the back of the lorry to replace his wounded escort. I offered to go with him, but since I didn't have my rifle we first drove to my barracks to get it.

Portobello barracks was almost deserted but we met a couple of fellows who gave us a hand with the loading. We'd almost finished getting the boxes on board when a second lorry drove up and we all pitched in and got that one loaded too. The drivers agreed to keep within sight of each other as they drove to the Four Courts, and one of the lads who'd helped to load the ammunition climbed up into the rear of the lorry with me and we took up firing positions on each side of the lorry to protect it in case we were ambushed.

We completed the trip without incident, but when our driver pulled up on the quays in front of the Four Courts so many bullets were ricocheting about that not even a sparrow could have survived in the crossfire. Some of our lads had already reached the perimeter of the building but the Irregulars were fighting desperately and our boys were running short of ammunition. We had to take the boxes of ammo right up to the fellows who were firing, but to avoid being hit by the Irregulars we had to crouch as low as possible as we ran forward. Our lads were tired and dirty, and they were as badly in need of a drink of water as they were of ammunition.

On our way back to Portobello barracks for another load of ammunition, we saw two empty tramcars stalled on the road ahead of us. They had been disconnected from the overhead electric lines and my mate in the back of the lorry said we'd better watch out for an ambush. As we slowed down to detour around the tramcars, I noticed an unusually well-dressed civilian walking along the pavement. As we approached him he put a cigarette into his mouth and reached into his pocket for a match. Instead of a match, however, he pulled out a revolver and fired two rounds at us before dashing down a side street. It was an old IRA trick which had often been used against the Black and Tans and I still admire how well he pulled it off. I fired at him but with the swerving of the lorry my shot went wild and the gunman kept on running. The second lorry which had been following us at a distance increased its speed and its escort also fired at the fleeing gunman but failed to bring him down.

As the second lorry caught up with us and drew alongside, we learned that our driver had been shot in the arm and was bleeding badly. Someone in the second lorry shouted to our driver to stop and let somebody else take the wheel but our driver wouldn't stop. Then a Whippet armoured car, attracted by the noise of the firing, drove into the road and followed us closely as our driver raced back to Portobello barracks where we carried him into the sick bay.

When we looked at our lorry we saw that a piece of wood about a foot and a half long had been torn out of the side very close to where I'd been standing. I'd had a lucky escape; the gunman's second shot had missed me by inches.

Paddy Lowe had also been escorting supplies to our lads attacking the Four Courts that day. Promoted to the rank of sergeant by that time, he and another fellow were standing in the rear of a big lorry in which two of our officers – both of them lieutenants – were riding up front with the driver. As they turned into Capel Street three shots were fired at the lorry. Each of the two officers in the front was wounded, and Paddy Lowe – God rest him – got a bullet in the heart. The driver, who escaped uninjured, drove straight to the Mater Hospital with the three wounded men. When they took Paddy Lowe down from the truck he was dead.

My heart broke when I heard that Paddy had been killed. We had been like brothers since the time he was a piper and I was a drummer in the Patrick Pearse Pipers Band in Liverpool. Both of us were Volunteers in the Liverpool Company of the IRA and as a result of the farm fires were sentenced to penal servitude; while I was given five years, Paddy got ten. He alone of all the other IRA prisoners in Dartmoor had remained steadfast with me to the end of both the work strikes and the hunger strike. We had joined the Irish army together at Beggar's Bush barracks, had belonged to the same company of the Dublin Guards, and had fought alongside each other at Kilkenny.

Paddy was a tall, powerfully built man, with the dark hair and good looks that appealed to the girls, yet he lived like a saint. Except for my father, there was no man I've ever met whom I more greatly admired and respected than Paddy Lowe.

Both the driver of the lorry and the two officers had noted where the shots had been fired from. They came from a haberdasher's shop in Capel Street owned by a family named Lemass. One of the sons, Seán Lemass, a member of the anti-Treatyite garrison fighting inside the Four Courts, later became Taoiseach (Prime Minister) of Ireland in June, 1959.[48] The other son, Noel Lemass, fled to the Isle of Man where he remained in hiding for the remainder of the Civil War which ended 'officially' in May, 1923. He returned to Ireland in July of that year thinking it was then safe for him to do so, but he was eventually caught and three months later his body was found in the Wicklow Hills.

After the capture of the Four Courts and the surrender of its garrison at 3.30pm on Friday afternoon, 30 June, many of the Irregulars still at large in Dublin set up a number of outposts and sniper positions throughout the city. In some instances, half a dozen or so Irregulars would seize a house, drive its occupants out into the street, and then pretend to control the area. As soon as we located such outposts it seldom took much effort to flush them out. We'd simply rush to the house in a tender, kick down the front door and arrest the startled 'defenders'.

Typical of the Irregulars' outposts in Dublin was the one occupied by Mattie Mullen, an old pal of mine who now lives in Dolphins Barn. Mattie told me he was one of a party that established an outpost in a house in Harcourt Terrace not far from another of their outposts across the canal. During the two weeks they occupied their outpost before they were attacked, the number of men staying in the house varied almost from day to day. Some days there might be twenty men; on other days as many as thirty or more. Soon after they had settled in, they thought they might run short of food so they went into Camden Street and raided the shops.

He said De Valera and some of his staff stayed at the outpost for four days and nights, but left the place only two days before it was attacked. At the time of the attack there were only fifteen men in the house. Two of our armoured cars drove right up to the place, one covering the front and the other covering the rear.

'Why didn't you fellows get out?' I asked him. 'Why didn't you go through the windows and make a run for it?'

'We couldn't,' he said, 'because the machine gun on the armoured car in front of the house reached over the low wall and fired a burst into the house.'

'And how long did the fight last?'

'In ten minutes we were finished,' he said.

'Was there much fighting?' I asked him.

'We had little to fight with,' he said.

'What about your rifles? Didn't you have a rifle, Mattie?'

'No,' he said. 'All I had was a .32 revolver. There were only four .32 revolvers among the fifteen of us.'

Then he went on to tell me what happened after they surrendered. 'We just walked out of the house and were taken to Portobello barracks where we were kept in the gymnasium for a couple of weeks before being sent to Kilmainham Prison for a few weeks more. We finally ended up in Gormanston Camp.'

'Did they beat you up?' I asked him, because I'd heard a lot of stories. 'Did they give you a rough time?'

'Ah, no,' he said. 'Some of the officers knew us quite well. Charlie Byrne, for example, knew me very well. They often gave us sweets and bars of chocolate. Gormanston: it was almost like a holiday camp. They treated us very decently, although just before we arrived at Gormanston some of our crowd had managed to cut their way through the wire fence, and escaped. One of them was Hughie Early. Do you remember him?'

'Yes,' I said. 'I remember him.'

9

IN ORDER TO PREVENT THE more strategically important points in Dublin from being seized by the anti-Treatyites, our two companies were split into several smaller groups and assigned to various locations throughout the city. On Friday afternoon, 30 June, I was one of a party sent to Amiens Street Station where we were billeted overnight in the compartments of an empty train.

It wasn't long before we were attacked by sporadic firing from some of the buildings overlooking the station. One particularly persistent sniper was firing from a nearby post office, and after breakfast on Saturday morning we decided to flush him out. We dashed across the street outside the station to take up firing positions, but a small crowd of onlookers gathered to watch us and we found that we had to get rid of the spectators before we could fire at the sniper.

While I was urging the onlookers to go home, a stout, elderly woman standing in the forefront of the crowd asked me, on hearing my accent, if I were English.

'No!' I snapped at her. 'I'm a Liverpool Volunteer.'

A few moments later I noticed her again but she had moved towards an alleyway on the far side of the crowd. She appeared to be studying me very closely and I became curious as to why she should be watching me so intently. Then to my surprise she made a slight but unmistakable gesture of signalling me to come closer.

'Do you know Paddy Daly?' she asked me when I went up to her.

'I do, well,' I said.

She slipped her hand into the bosom of her dress and drew out a long envelope and gave it to me.

'Don't give this to anyone but Paddy Daly,' she said.

I nodded my agreement and as casually as possible made my way back to the railway station where I asked an officer on the platform if I could see Paddy Daly.

'What do you want him for?' the officer asked.

'I have a special message for him,' I said.

'A message?' he said. 'Who are you?' I told him my name and then he led me to Paddy Daly whom I saw further down the platform.

'Who gave it to you?' Paddy Daly asked me when I handed him the long envelope.

'A woman,' I said. 'I don't know her name, but she was a stout, elderly looking woman.'

'Come in here,' he said indicating with a gesture that we were to follow him into an empty office leading off the platform. He walked straight over to a table beneath a huge window, opened up the envelope and took out a street map with little crosses marked in red ink.

The two officers looked at the map for a moment, and then glancing at me, began to grin: the little red crosses marked the location of snipers in the vicinity of Amiens Street Station. The officer who'd led me to Paddy Daly opened up the big window and spread out the map on the table. 'There you are, Paddy,' he said looking out the window. 'There he is! And there's another one, over there!'

The two officers picked up their rifles, and taking aim carefully, they fired almost simultaneously. As they commenced firing, I quietly slipped out of the room and returned to join the rest of my party.

I was most impressed by the shrewdness of that elderly woman who'd given me the envelope to deliver to Paddy Daly. She had evidently gone through the surrounding area of Amiens Street Station and noted every sniper's position, marking them on the map. She must surely have known by sight, at least, some of the soldiers in our party, almost all of whom were Dubliners and had belonged to the Dublin Brigade of the IRA. But she had decided to give the map to someone who didn't know her so that there wouldn't be any repercussions, and I, apparently, fitted the bill!

Later that day (Saturday 1 July) a lieutenant gathered up ten of us scattered about the platforms of Amiens Street Station and told us to follow him to Moran's Hotel which was located on the north-east corner of the junction between Talbot Street and Lower Gardiner Street. As we went down the steps from the station into Amiens

Street we were warned by a couple of lads on the steps to expect heavy sniping as we approached Moran's Hotel because it was a strongly defended anti-Treatyite outpost.

As we entered Talbot Street from its eastern end and moved westwards along it, five soldiers from our group crossed over to the south side of the street while the rest of us remained on the north side. The lieutenant was at the head of our party and I was positioned next but one behind him. As we approached the hotel, the anti-Treatyites within the building began firing at us, and the soldier leading the party advancing on the south side of Talbot Street was the first of our group of ten to return the fire, shooting at a hotel window opening onto Talbot Street. Then the soldier who'd fired the first shots dashed across to tell us that he could see a land mine in the road outside the hotel, and our lieutenant ran back with him to take a look for himself. In the centre of Lower Gardiner Street and in line with a large window on the ground floor of the hotel was a black box about twelve inches long, twelve inches wide, and six inches high. A heavy, black cable led from the hotel window to the black box.

The lieutenant fired a few shots at an open window facing Talbot Street and then returning to our party on the north side of the street said to me and the lad in front, 'We'll rush it ... watch out for the land mine when we get to the door!'

The three of us, led by the lieutenant, dashed past the open window and up the steps to the hotel door. It was locked, so while the lieutenant put his shoulder to the door, the other soldier and I smashed at it with our rifle butts until it flew open. The lieutenant, who was the first through the door, ran into the lobby and then into the front room on the left – the room to which the cable from the land mine led – while the soldier who was in front of me dashed into the room on the right. I ran to the room further back on the right-hand side of the short hallway and kicking open the door shouted, 'Surrender!'

Nobody answered but when I stepped inside the room, a peculiar atmosphere about the place caused me to stop instantly. I looked carefully around me but the room was empty except for a clean-topped bureau and a double bed covered with a clean white sheet. Another soldier dashed into the room to join me, but he, too, felt there was something uncanny about the room and we both stood stock still for a few moments before dashing across the floor to a window on the far side of the room. A shade was drawn over the window and when my mate let the shade up, we found ourselves looking into the back yard of the hotel. We remained at the window until the rest of our party, who had raced into the hotel after we smashed open its front door, had searched the entire hotel and then the yard. After they completed their search outside they shouted back to us that all the Irregulars had gone.

We all returned to the front door to explode the land mine, but a crowd had already begun to gather along the far side of Gardiner Street and we had to get the crowd out of the way before we could explode the mine. The crowd was so reluctant to move, however, that we even tried firing warning shots over their heads but it wasn't until additional troops arrived on the scene that we were able to push back the crowd. The captain of the newly arrived troops, together with our own lieutenant, then fired several shots at the mine in order to explode it, but since it refused to go off we finally concluded it was a dummy.

While I was helping to push the crowd back to a safe distance I felt a fellow in the crowd studying me. Our eyes met and we stared silently at each other. I recognised him as Donal Mulhall, a former member of the Liverpool Company, and shook my head sadly. He was wearing a civilian suit of tweeds with a Red Cross band tied around his right arm – no knapsack of first-aid supplies, or anything like that. I felt certain he was one of the gang that had escaped through the back door of Moran's Hotel. He didn't speak when I recognised him; he simply walked away. It was the first time I'd seen him since my arrest in Liverpool.

I'd first met Donal when I was serving my apprenticeship at Marsdens and he arrived from Dublin to serve his time with the firm. His arrival at Marsdens was unusual in two respects: he was over sixteen years of age and a Catholic. He had a very gentle nature and appeared to be a more intellectual type than most of the apprentices. I took a great interest in him, and after several lengthy conversations with him, I asked him to join the Volunteers and he became a member of the Liverpool Company.

After the land mine had proved to be a dummy, the captain placed a guard on Moran's Hotel and the lieutenant collected our group and we returned to Amiens Street Station. From the outside, the hotel appeared undamaged except for bullet holes in the brickwork which had been caused by a Whippet firing at the snipers. Inside the hotel, however, one could see a large hole in the roof.

Years later I was told of a published version of the episode at Moran's Hotel which claimed that the hotel's garrison surrendered to our troops. But none of the Irregulars surrendered. There was nobody in the hotel when we searched it; the Irregulars had run away.

About eleven o'clock that night a lieutenant took a party of about ten of us to patrol some of the streets between Amiens Street Station and Mountjoy Square in a search for anti-Treatyite outposts. There wasn't a soul abroad in the vicinity of Amiens Street when we emerged from the station, and we felt a rare, uncanny quietness hanging over Dublin. We cut across the road in front of the station and then advanced very slowly down Amiens Street in extended order, keeping a tight grip on our rifles in case we were suddenly attacked. We didn't enter any of the houses along the way, but our eyes searched the dark silent buildings for unclosed windows and doors left slightly ajar from which the muzzle of a rifle or a machine gun might suddenly emerge. It was almost midnight when we finally reached Mountjoy Square having scouted slowly and silently along the way which was supposed to be cleared of anti-Treatyites.

When we reached Mountjoy Square, our lieutenant signalled us to halt and gave instructions – which were whispered along from one man to the next – that we were to take off our boots, tie their laces together, and sling them over our shoulders. Then we moved down Gardiner Street, crouching low and keeping as close as possible to the walls, until we came to one particular house where our lieutenant quietly tapped on the door. After a few moments the door was opened by the lady of the house who beckoned us to enter and we all filed in. When we were all safely inside, the lieutenant told us we were to remain in the house until shortly before dawn, and having posted a sentry we should be able to get some rest. Then he turned us over to the lady of the house. 'You can sleep upstairs,' she said to us. 'Just take your time ... up to a room on the top floor.' The woman led us upstairs into a front room (facing the street) on the third or fourth floor of the house.

When we were all inside the room, the lieutenant told us to lie down on the floor and try to get some sleep, but the room wasn't large enough to accommodate all of us comfortably. I was still on my feet trying to slacken my bandolier when there was a sudden flash in front of me and a shot rang out.

'Oh my God!' I said. 'It's me!' And I could feel the blood trickling down my face and I started to pray.

'Jasus! Seán's hit!' I heard someone say. 'Who did it ... ? What eedjit ...?'

I sank down on my knees and a lad beside me lit a match. I wiped my face and then looked at my hands to see the blood ... but all I saw was sweat. Only sweat, thanks be to God.

At daybreak we all got up quickly, and carrying our boots crept down the stairs. When the lady of the house (who'd been watching at the window) gave us the 'all clear,' we slipped out of the building and stole back to Amiens Street Station, making a careful detour around a suspected machine gun post.

By noon on Sunday, 2 July, the attempts made by the Archbishop of Dublin and the Lord Mayor to negotiate a peace settlement between the Provisional Government and the executive of the anti-Treatyite forces had clearly failed, and the government was forced to make the fateful decision to attack the anti-Treatyite headquarters in Sackville Street.

Following the destruction of their original headquarters in the Four Courts, the anti-Treatyites had seized a number of buildings (including several well-known hotels) in a section along the east side of Sackville Street and had established their headquarters in the

Hammam Hotel. But in seizing the hotels and establishing themselves in a barricaded position, the Anti-Treatyite leadership of Oscar Traynor, Cathal Brugha and Austin Stack made the same tactical error as the leaders of the Rising in 1916. They had needlessly isolated themselves and late on Sunday afternoon, 2 July, the National Army moved in on them.

Ten of us under the command of a lieutenant left Amiens Street Station and, detouring through West Gardiner Street, Gardiner Place, and North Great George's Street, advanced up Parnell Street (formerly named Great Britain Street). We moved cautiously along Parnell Street because of the sporadic firing in the vicinity, slipping from door to door – five of us along one side of the street and six on the other – until we reached the junction of Parnell Street and Upper Sackville Street.

On the south-east corner of the junction was a well-known tobacconist's shop in which we had planned to establish our command post, but when the lieutenant (who was leading the party on the south side of Parnell Street) discovered that the doors of the shop immediately east of the tobacconist's were heavily barricaded, he and the two lads behind him smashed the windows and fired several volleys into the front room of the shop. The party on the south side of the street then climbed in through the broken windows, and when we saw that they were safely inside the shop, we crossed over and joined them.

In a wall at the back of the shop we found a hole – big enough for a man to crawl through – which led into the next building, and while five of our lads blazed away at the hole, the rest of us raced upstairs to search the rooms above the shop. When I reached the top floor I kicked open a door leading into a room on the corner of Parnell Street and Upper Sackville Street, and dashing inside I discovered a sniper lying full length on a table in front of a window overlooking what is now Parnell Square. He was resting on some pillows with his rifle aimed out of the window and his fingers closed around the trigger.

I shouted at him to surrender, and in case he was tempted to swing his rifle around at me, warned him not to make any sudden movements. Hearing my shouts, one of our lads came dashing into the room and the two of us covered the sniper with our rifles as we waited for him to surrender. But the prone figure remained so silent and still that we finally realised that he was dead.

We edged closer to get a better look at the poor fellow and to take away his rifle, but we froze when we saw that the top and front of the sniper's head was a mass of red feathers. As we stared at the dead man we concluded that while he was sniping from his position at the window, the crew of one of our Whippets must have spotted him and sent a burst of machine-gun fire in his direction – the bullets cutting through the pillows and the top of the sniper's head. When we examined the dead sniper's rifle, we found a live round in the breech. He had been killed just as he was about to fire. My mate searched for a revolver on him, but didn't find one, and then we called down for the St John's ambulance men who came and took away the corpse. When we examined the room more completely we saw that the sniper had made two small holes in the walls by loosening some of the bricks. From one hole he had been able to cover Parnell Street, and from the other, Cavendish Row. His tragic mistake was to expose himself to the machine gunner in the Whippet against whose firepower he had no chance.

My mate and I went downstairs to rejoin the rest of our group who were blasting their way through the buildings in the Findlater block. It was a dangerous, nerve-wracking task as we searched for the hole in the wall that would lead into the next building. The holes had been made in the walls by the Irregulars who'd torn away the bricks until they'd made gaps large enough to permit them to crawl from one house to the next along the entire length of the block between Parnell Street and Findlater Place. As we made our way through the buildings we sometimes found ourselves being shot at from behind and realised we had bypassed the Irregulars. Sometimes we even fired in error at our own lads as we raced from room to room searching frantically for those holes torn in the brick work.

As darkness began to fall before we were able to clear the block of Irregulars, the lieutenant recalled us all to the front room of the shop on Parnell Street. We expected that during the night the Irregulars would try to return to the building so the lieutenant arranged for us to take turns guarding the hole in the rear of the shop.

Before I kipped down for the night, some of the lads told me that a posh-looking Englishman had been asking for my whereabouts saying that he wanted to meet me. Someone pointed him out, and when I saw the spats, kid gloves, bowler hat, and tightly-rolled umbrella, I couldn't imagine who in hell he was or why he wanted to see me. Nevertheless, I went over to him and introduced myself.

'John,' he said, 'I've been looking all over Dublin for you ... your parents are worried sick about you ... they say you haven't written to them, and with all the fighting in Dublin they wonder if you're still alive. When they heard I was coming over, they asked me to try and find you. Now you're coming to my hotel with me and you're going to sit down and write a letter to your mother.'

I thought I'd seen his face somewhere before, but it wasn't until we got to his hotel that I realised he was one of the McDermotts, a family that lived in Hemer Terrace, Bootle, not far from where we lived at No. 149 Rimrose Road. His parents were good friends of my mother and father, and I'd often been teased at home for being fond of his younger sister, Delia. In his hotel room, McDermott gave me a pad of writing paper and told me he wasn't going to let me leave until I'd written the letter but that I wasn't to tell my mother about the fighting. He said he was returning to Liverpool shortly and would deliver the letter personally.

It wasn't until a long time afterwards that I learned that McDermott was, in fact, an Oriel House[49] plainclothes man. While pretending to be an English businessman or journalist, he wandered around Dublin taking notes of the activities and dispositions of the anti-Treatyite forces.

Early next morning (Monday 3 July) the lieutenant took me and three others to scout for Irregulars who might have infiltrated the block, but before we set off he warned the rest to be sure not to mistake us for Irregulars when we returned. We'd no sooner left our comrades and started our search than a number of shots rang out and echoed through the building as the Irregulars heard our approach. The five of us stuck together because if we separated – some going up a stairway while the others went down – we might easily have fired at each other in the confusion of searching for the Irregulars in the darkened interior of the buildings.

It became a nightmarish task as we slowly made our way from one room to another, searching for the holes that would lead into the next building. Each time we came to a hole in one of the walls we fired a steady hail of bullets through the hole until we thought it was safe enough for us to climb into the next room or building. Finally a couple of Irregulars shouted to us to stop firing because they wished to surrender. We immediately stopped firing and when the fellows came through a couple of our lads confiscated their .45 revolvers and ammunition. The lieutenant detailed the two lads to escort the prisoners to the shop in Parnell Street with instructions that the prisoners were to be placed under guard in a lorry parked near the shop.

When our lads came back we continued fighting our way through the Findlater block and it wasn't long before another couple of Irregulars surrendered. Then it was my turn and that of the fourth soldier in our party to relieve the prisoners of their revolvers and I became the owner of a .45 calibre short-barrelled Webley and a small quantity of ammunition. The two prisoners were escorted to Parnell Street by the same two lads who'd escorted the previous prisoners and when they returned we resumed the fight.

In one particular room, however, we ran into such steady firing from an escape hole that we became alarmed at the possible number of Irregulars on the other side of the wall. We returned volley for volley until suddenly we heard a woman's voice from the other side of the wall shouting, 'Stop firing! Stop firing! Don't shoot ... I'm a Red Cross nurse. I'm coming through!' We immediately ceased firing and after a pause watched with great curiosity as a woman came crawling through the hole in the wall. When she emerged we could see she was wearing an improvised nurse's uniform with a red cross stitched on the front of her white apron, and as she straightened up we saw that she was an attractive, fine-looking woman.

'Don't touch me!' she said as she came forward. 'I'm a Red Cross nurse.'

Despite her protest, however, one of our lads shrewdly tapped the deep pocket on the right-hand side of her apron.

'How dare you!' she shouted at him. 'I'm a woman! Don't you dare search me! Don't you touch me!'

But the lad thrust his hand into her pocket regardless and pulled out a revolver – and we all stood still as we watched a thin wisp of smoke curl out of its barrel.

Our lieutenant told the same two lads who'd taken the other prisoners to the little shop in Parnell Street to take her along too and to be sure they saw her placed in the lorry. A couple of the lads who'd belonged to the Dublin Brigade of the Old IRA recognised her as having been a member of the Cumann na mBan. They said that her married name was O'Carroll, and that during the Tan War her husband had held up – or tried to hold up – a post office in the name of the IRA, although he had nothing to do with the IRA. He was caught, but the Dublin Metropolitan Police knew he wasn't a Volunteer and the poor fellow was sentenced to penal servitude. The name rang a bell; I remembered an O'Carroll among a group of convicts brought over from Dublin to do their penal servitude in Dartmoor Prison because there was no room for them in Irish prisons, and that he'd robbed – or tried to rob – with a revolver while posing as an IRA man.

When Nurse O'Carroll's escort returned, we fought on – upstairs and downstairs through the buildings eventually reaching the premises containing Findlater's stores at the end of the block, where we found ourselves on a first floor landing from which stairs led down to a store-room into which the Irregulars had retreated. The six or seven steps of the stairway led to another landing about four feet wide before a further six or seven steps led directly into the store-room at the bottom. We soon realised that the Irregulars had retreated into an almost impregnable position; while they remained in complete darkness, we were caught in the light coming from the head of the stairway. Each time we as much as put a foot on the stairs the Irregulars fired a volley up the stairs – and we knew we'd have to reach the landing below us before we would be in an effective firing position. We tried firing at them from every angle possible – lying down and crouching – but were unable to make any progress.

The lieutenant called me, and explaining that he was returning through the building to Parnell Street, told me to guard the corner of an L-shaped corridor behind us. There were several doors leading off the corridor in both directions and the lieutenant warned me to look out for Irregulars who might try to encircle us. He said that on his way back he'd call out so I'd recognise him, but until he returned I spent a nerve-wracking time glancing first along one corridor and then the other, hoping none of our own lads would step into the hallway.

When he returned, the lieutenant decided that we'd have to leap to the landing below us and then try to rush the store-room. On his signal we all leapt together and although we were caught in the light, we all managed to reach the landing without being hit. No sooner had we reached the landing, however, than an egg bomb was lobbed at us, but it struck the banister rail and fell straight down into an open sack of sugar on the ground floor. Fortunately, the sack had been opened with the sides rolled back to enable one to scoop out the sugar, so the egg bomb, which landed in the sugar, didn't explode.

Our position on the landing was exposed to the Irregulars who kept up such a steady fusillade that our lieutenant realised we'd best get back to the top landing. 'Now!' he shouted, and the five of us leapt back. If anyone had stumbled – or even hesitated – we would have fallen over each other and been riddled by the Irregulars down below.

When we caught our breath again, the lieutenant told us that we'd still have to rush the store-room; that we'd jump down to the landing once more but that we'd keep on going – firing as we went – until we stormed our way through to the store-room.

We shouted at the Irregulars to surrender but when they showed no sign of yielding we jumped down to the landing once more and opened up with a withering blast of rifle fire. Still firing, we charged down the rest of the stairs and stormed through the barricade of boxes and crates blocking the entrance. When we got inside the store-room it was so dark and silent that we had to light matches as we searched for the dead and wounded whom we expected to find lying about us. As we groped around the store-room we didn't find any Irregulars but one of our lads discovered a door which – to our surprise when we opened it – led directly into Findlater Place (part of which is now known as Cathal Brugha Street). We realised then that we'd finally driven the Irregulars right out of the block: that those who had retreated to the store-room had fled through the side door. We dashed outside to search for them but Findlater Place was deserted.

But above the door through which the Irregulars had escaped, we found a long pole stretching horizontally over the width of the pavement, and from the pole hung a Red Cross flag. It was made of a beautiful white linen tablecloth on which broad red ribbons had been sown, and when I took it down, I folded it up and put it in my knapsack. The other lads suggested that it should either be kept as a souvenir of the Irregulars' treachery or that it be sent to Dev as a reminder of his sojourn in Sir Patrick Dun's Hospital![50]

We were still brooding over the Irregulars' treachery in flying a Red Cross flag when we returned inside the store-room and saw the number of empty shells and cartridges that littered the floor. Our minds went back to Mrs O'Carroll whom we had captured earlier, and we agreed that we ought to have shot her because had she succeeded in her trickery she would have returned to the Irregulars and told them our exact strength.

The store-room was in complete darkness when we closed the side door leading to Findlater Place, so our lieutenant sent one of the lads to buy a few candles in Parnell Street and then went off himself to report that the Findlater block was cleared of Irregulars. With the aid of lighted candles the lieutenant and some of the rest of the boys who'd been guarding the shop in Parnell Street made a thorough search through every room in the Findlater block looking for dead or wounded Irregulars but failed to find any. We felt very pleased with ourselves in having gained control of the Findlater buildings, and after we lit a few candles in the store-room we barricaded the door leading into Findlater Place. The boxes of provisions stacked against the walls were especially tempting since we were so hungry and thirsty, and we helped ourselves to the tinned food and bottles of mineral water lying around us.

One of the lads found a nearby room whose walls were lined with bottles of wine and spirits, and for the sheer hell of it I fired at some of the bottles. It was more fun than a cockshy at a fairground! None of us would touch the bottles of spirits, but I washed down some biscuits with a couple of good swigs of Wincarnis. One fellow found a barrel of stout and, pleading that he was 'dried up,' helped himself to the stout. Unfortunately he took too much of the stuff, so we took away his rifle, and telling him not to return until he'd slept it off, sent him back to the shop in Parnell Street. Dusk was then falling, so we posted sentries for the night and caught some badly needed sleep.

The following morning (Tuesday, 4 July) I was sent to the top-floor room where I'd found the dead sniper two days earlier, with another soldier – a Lewis gunner – detailed to join me. When we reached the room, we placed the Lewis gun on the table near the window so as to be able to cover the houses on the far (or west) side of Upper Sackville Street. There was, at that time, considerable firing in the street below us, but no shots were aimed at us.

On the far side of Upper Sackville Street, and at an oblique angle from our position, there was a building with the letters YMCA in large white capitals affixed to the walls on a level with the second floor of the building. Partly out of devilment, but largely out of boredom, the Lewis gunner and I argued as to which of us could knock the letters YMCA off the building. Eventually the Lewis gunner bet me a packet of cigarettes that I couldn't hit the top left-hand pane in the top left-hand window of the building carrying the letters. It was a difficult target because of its angle from us but I bet the Lewis gunner two packets of cigarettes that I'd knock out the entire pane. Putting down my rifle, I swung the Lewis gun around, fired a couple of

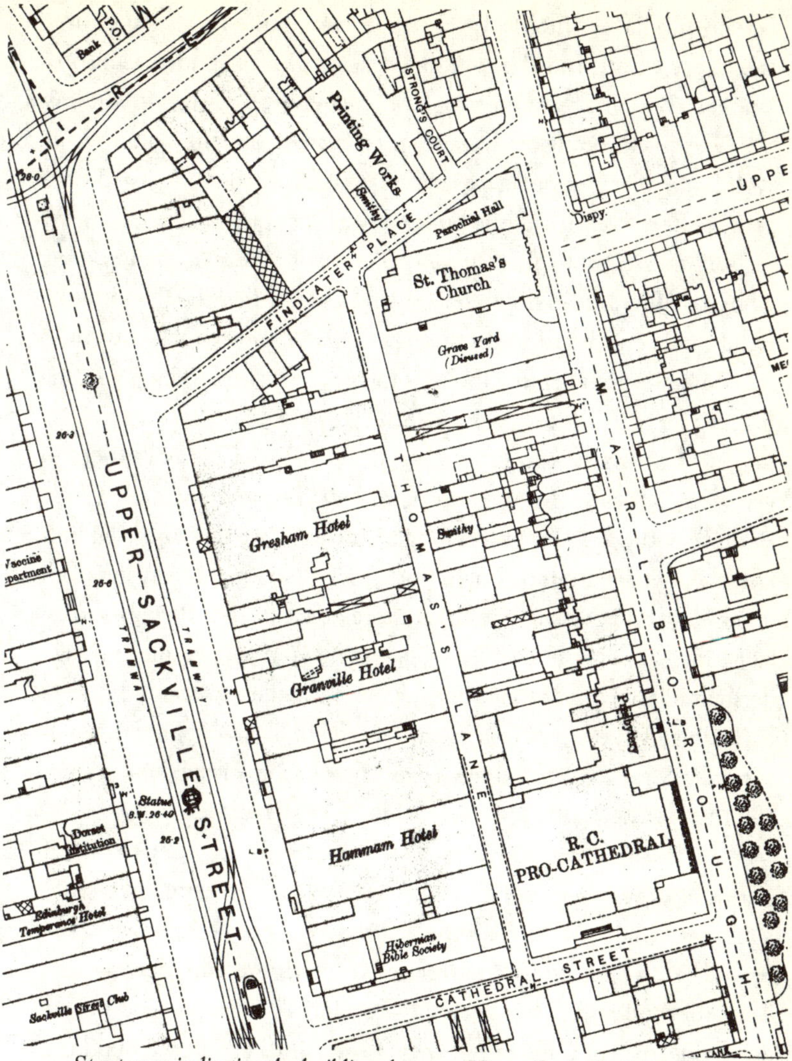

Street map indicating the buildings between Upper Sackville Street (now O'Connell Street) and Marlborough Street, 1922. (Used with kind permission of the Ordnance Survey Office, Phoenix Park, Dublin. Permit No. 6619).

short bursts, and blasted all the glass out of the pane!

While we were looking at the window and arguing about our marksmanship, we noticed a puff of smoke rising out of the space where the pane had been, but when the smoke quickly dissipated, we wondered, if, perhaps, I'd hit a gas pipe. I told my mate I'd find out for certain and having fitted a whole new drum in the Lewis gun, I fired the entire drum into the window. Jasus! All of a sudden clouds of smoke – followed by tongues of flames – billowed out of the window.

We quickly pulled the Lewis gun away from the window sill, wondering if any of our own lads were inside the building we'd fired at. If, on the other hand, the building was occupied by Irregulars, we realised they'd probably try to escape from the rear of the building. The two of us agreed not to tell anyone we'd caused the fire, but that we should send word to those of our lads whom we knew were in Moore Street to be on the lookout for any Irregulars trying to escape from the rear of Upper Sackville Street.

I ran downstairs to the shop and when I told the boys there to get word across to Moore Street, one of them volunteered to go. Because of the amount of shooting in Sackville Street, I expected him to make a wide detour through North Great George's Street and Gardiner Row, and crossing the street there, to go around Parnell Square to Moore Street. But the lad who volunteered to take the message decided to save time by crossing Upper Sackville Street more directly. Taking a terrible risk of being hit by the bullets whipping through Sackville Street, he darted like a hare first to the Parnell Monument and then to the bank on the west side.

When he returned he told us he'd passed the message to one of our officers who'd then rushed his men to the rear doors in Moore Lane, and that the YMCA rooms had, indeed, been occupied by a few Irregulars and that they'd surrendered in Moore Lane having fled from the building. The Lewis gunner and I said how relieved we were to learn that none of our own crowd had been in the building, but we didn't let on that we'd caused the fire.[51]

That evening, while my mate and I were keeping watch in the room where we'd found the dead sniper, our lieutenant came to take us through the buildings to Findlater's store-room – my mate carrying his Lewis gun while I carried the drums of ammunition.

Then, as dusk began to fall, the three of us slipped upstairs to a small living-room whose window commanded an unobstructed view down the length of Thomas' Lane all the way from Findlater

Place to Cathedral Street. Thomas' Lane ran (as it does today) between the buildings on the east side of Upper Sackville Street (now O'Connell Street) and those on the west side of Marlborough Street. From our vantage point, nothing could cross Thomas' Lane without the Lewis gunner and me seeing it. Before leaving, the lieutenant instructed us to guard Findlater's and to keep a careful watch on the backs of the buildings in Upper Sackville Street, especially the rear exits of the Hammam and Grenville hotels.

Satisfied with the commanding position of the room and its window, my mate and I went down to the store-room on the ground floor where we made sure the side door leading into Findlater Place was strongly barricaded against re-entry from the outside, and then took back with us a supply of biscuits and mineral waters. When we returned to the living-room we set up the Lewis gun on a table in front of the window and checked to make sure that its drums of ammunition were filled and ready for use. We soon found, however, that the arrangement of the table against the window in such a small room was an awkward one and didn't leave us enough space to manoeuvre, so we finally decided to move the table away from the window and simply sit on a couple of chairs in front of the window.

We just sat there, my mate on the left and me on the right, with our rifles between our knees, the magazines fully loaded and the safety catches 'off'. We had placed the Lewis gun against the wall in the left-hand corner of the room – only a couple of feet away from my mate who could easily reach for it if we needed it in a hurry. Whenever our backsides started to get numb from sitting on the hard wooden chairs, we knelt on one knee on the floor, but sitting or kneeling we kept a constant watch on Thomas' Lane.

With nightfall we became particularly alert for anyone trying to slip into Thomas' Lane from the buildings in Upper Sackville Street, because of the possibility that some of the Irregulars might try to infiltrate the Findlater Building. We were prepared to shoot anyone who tried to do so.

Later in the night we agreed to take turns catnapping on the floor beneath the window. Since there was no clock in the room and neither of us had a watch we had no way of timing each other's rest; whenever the one on watch began to feel drowsy, he woke up the one who was sleeping. I was fast asleep during one of those spells when I felt my mate tapping urgently on my shoulder and whispering for me to wake up. He was on one knee, looking out of the window, and as I grabbed my rifle, I realised by the amount of thin light coming from the east that dawn was breaking. It was Wednesday morning, 5 July 1922.

I wondered what the Lewis gunner had seen as I crouched beside him while he strained his eyes against the weak lights.

'There's a sniper on the roof,' he whispered.

'I see him now,' I said. 'He's standing up ... let's fire together.' We each took careful aim and fired almost simultaneously but the sniper remained standing.

'We missed!' said my mate, so we fired again.

Then I saw a second figure. 'There's two of them on the roof!' I said. Aiming carefully I fired a round at the second figure. My first shot failed to bring him down so I fired three more shots in rapid succession.

Dawn was breaking fast and as the light increased we could see the figures silhouetted more clearly against the sky. Suddenly we stopped firing. We could clearly identify the two 'snipers'. They were, in fact, two statues on the roof of the Pro-Cathedral!

My mate and I looked at each other and wondered if what we'd done was a sacrilege. We said we hoped that Archbishop Byrne would not find out what we'd done to his statues, but agreed we should tell the priest in confession that we'd shot at his statues ... just in case we'd committed a sin!

It was then my turn to keep watch and let the Lewis gunner get some sleep.

Some time later in the morning when we were both wide awake and watching for any movement in Thomas' Lane, we fell to arguing as to which of us could hit a window in Bolgers, a shop on Cathedral Street clearly visible at the far end of Thomas' Lane. We agreed not to shoot at the shop windows, but only those on the first, second, and third floors above the shop. We began blazing away with our rifles, but at such a long range we couldn't be certain that our bullets were hitting their targets so eventually we gave up. Then I saw a better target. About seventy yards from our position at the window, a heavy wooden beam jutted out from a loft on the east side of Thomas' Lane and from the end of the beam hung a chain to which a ball and hook were attached – all part of a hoist for raising goods to the loft from drays driven into the lane.

We bet cigarettes as to which of us could hit the metal ball (six or eight inches in diameter) at the end of the chain immediately above the hook. This time there was no argument as to whether or not we'd hit the target, because each time a bullet hit the ball, we could see the hook and chain jerk under the impact. I was a good shot and able to hit the ball every time I fired, but my mate, the Lewis gunner, wasn't as accurate, and although our competition helped to pass the time, he eventually lost interest and stopped shooting.

Later on in the day when we noticed smoke billowing into Thomas' Lane from the rear of one of the buildings facing Upper Sackville Street – about two-thirds the way down the lane – we quickly settled into firing positions because we expected some action if the Irregulars were forced out of the burning building and into the lane. We watched the clouds of smoke become increasingly heavier at the far (or south) end of the lane, but there was no smoke at all at our end. In fact, the air was so perfectly clear at the northern end of the lane we thought that it was very likely that the Irregulars, instead of stumbling into the smoke-filled section of Thomas' Lane and taking their chances there, would work their way northwards through the buildings and fight it out at our end. Both my mate and I then fell silent; we simply knelt together in front of the window with our rifles between our knees and made sure our magazines were full.

We quietly watched the smoke pouring out of the building burning on the east side of Sackville Street and felt the mounting tension as we waited for the inevitable appearance of the Irregulars breaking out.

'There's one!' my mate said suddenly.

'I see him!' I replied as I saw an arm emerge from a doorway on the right-hand side of the lane. The arm, around which was fastened a Red Cross armlet, waved up and down three or four times like a railway signal. Then the arm was pulled in and a head which quickly turned from one side to the other appeared momentarily. The head ducked back and in the next instant a man wearing a Red Cross armlet sprang from the doorway and dashed across the lane. I had his head within the sights of my rifle from the moment he left the door until he disappeared through the doorway across the lane, but I did not pull the trigger because of the armlet he wore.

As soon as he had safely crossed the lane, another arm wearing a Red Cross armlet waved up and down from the doorway on the right-hand side of the lane and a second man followed the first across the lane. Then about four or five more men – each wearing a Red Cross armlet – emerged one at a time (but without waving their arms up and down) and dashed across. As soon as one man made it safely across the lane, the next one followed. I instinctively kept each one of them in my sights as he crossed the lane, swinging my rifle back to cover the next one as he emerged from the west side.

Then, after a pause of a minute or so, about five more men – all wearing Red Cross armlets – bolted into the lane, each man a couple of paces behind the one in front.

'Look!' said my mate as the first two men could be more distinctly seen. 'Rifles under their coats!'

I focused my attention on the second man who, when he was almost halfway across, gave a leap and the sides of his trench coat flew back to reveal very clearly a rifle he was carrying underneath the coat. Then I saw rifle butts sticking out beneath the coat hems of the third and fourth man, and it was reasonable to suppose that every damned one of them carried a rifle under his coat as he crossed Thomas' Lane.

We could have shot them all. I had only to drop the first one – in the second group of four or five – and the rest would have tumbled over him as they scurried across. It would then have been quite easy for my mate and me to pick them off as they sprawled on the ground. But we held our fire because each Irregular who entered Thomas'

Lane from the rear of Upper Sackville Street wore a Red Cross armlet.

We expected more Irregulars to follow the others so we kept our rifles aimed at the doorway from which the other men had emerged until we began to doubt if, indeed, any more would come out. Then we began to wonder where the Irregulars who'd escaped across Thomas' Lane were, and what they were up to. If they got into Marlborough Street they could either make good their escape by mingling with the pedestrians there or, if they chose to do so, mow down any unsuspecting soldiers they might encounter. There was also the possibility that the Irregulars might barricade some of the houses in Marlborough Street and establish another outpost. We discussed the possible courses of action the Irregulars might have taken and agreed that our lads in Marlborough Street should be warned. My mate, the Lewis gunner, couldn't leave his machine gun, so I went downstairs, out the store-room side door, and ran through Findlater Place to Marlborough Street.

There were a few civilians walking unconcernedly along Marlborough Street because, unlike Sackville Street, it was relatively safe from rifle fire, but there were no soldiers at the junction of Findlater Place and Marlborough Street and I began to think I was too late. Then I saw a soldier on the west side of Marlborough Street about eight houses south of the corner and I ran up to him and told him that a party of Irregulars had escaped across Thomas' Lane into the rear of the buildings on Marlborough Street, and despite their Red Cross armlets they carried rifles under their coats. I told him to take cover and keep a careful watch until I got some more men. I ran further on until I found another soldier near the Pro-Cathedral and told him the same. A couple more soldiers turned the corner close by and I told one of them to get his officer into Marlborough Street as quickly as possible, and within moments he returned on the double with his officer. When I told the officer what had been happening, he said he'd go and get some more men to cope with the situation and then he let me return to Findlater's building when I told him I wanted to get back there because my mate was on his own.

The four soldiers I'd met had already moved into the doorways as I ran back up Marlborough Street, but when I turned the corner into Findlater Place I was surprised to see the Lewis gunner standing outside the door of Findlater's store-room.

'Any more come out?' I shouted to him as we met at the entrance to Thomas' Lane. I remember his answer very clearly.

'Only one,' he replied. 'Cathal Brugha. He was shot ... they took him away.'

I asked him no further questions because his laconic – even cryptic – reply was intended to avoid directly implicating himself or anyone else in the fatality. It was an IRA custom which we maintained in the National Army. No one boasted of a victim.

The two of us moved towards the doorway in Thomas' Lane from which we'd seen the Irregulars emerge. Just before we reached the doorway I saw a handful – about eight – empty brass cartridges lying on the ground in the centre of the lane.

I bent down, picked them up, and was examining them when my mate said, 'They're from his gun.'

'An automatic,' I said as I studied the rims of the empty 9mm cases. 'I suppose it was a "Peter-the-Painter".[52] I'll keep these as a souvenir.' (A few days later when I told Bridie Mullen – an old flame of mine from Liverpool who was then living in Dublin – that I had the spent cartridges from Cathal Brugha's gun, she asked me to give her some as a keepsake and I gave her four of them).

The Lewis gunner and I remained in Thomas' Lane for the next hour or so watching the progress of the fire consuming the hotel buildings on the east side of Upper Sackville Street. As the fire steadily spread closer to us the lane became increasingly obscured by smoke and eventually the flames threatened to jump across Findlater Place to the Findlater block. When the heat became unbearable and we were sure no more Irregulars could possibly have survived in the burning buildings, my mate saw no point in us trying to guard the lane any longer so we returned to the little room above Findlater's store-room to pick up the Lewis gun and the drums of ammunition. The Lewis gun was still lying where I'd last seen it – against the wall in the corner of the small living-room. It hadn't been used.

My mate carried the Lewis gun while I carried the drums as we went downstairs again through the provisions store-room, into Findlater Place and then turned east to Marlborough Street. (Had we not had to lug the Lewis gun and the fully loaded drums of ammunition with us – in addition to carrying our rifles and bandoliers – we might have returned to the little shop in Parnell Street by way of the holes knocked in the walls of the buildings in the Findlater block.) On the corner of Marlborough Street there were two civilians, one of whom ran up to me and begged me to help save a couple of horses in a stable off Findlater Place. I said that it was too dangerous for anyone to go back, but he kept pleading, saying that the horses in Findlater's stables would be roasted alive unless they were released. Finally I relented, and giving my drums of ammo to the Lewis gunner, I asked him to wait for me at the corner until I returned.

The civilian showed me where the horses were stabled, but a heavily locked iron gate (only a few feet away from the side door of Findlater's store-room) prevented easy entry to the stables. As soon as I saw the locked gate I said to the civilian, 'To hell with it!' and turned to leave, but the fellow insisted I try to help him force the gate open.

'Stand back, then!' I said, and when he retreated a safe distance I took my rifle and fired several rapid shots at the lock. Then when I clouted the lock with my rifle butt the gate flew open and I told the civilian – who'd been joined by the other civilian from the corner of Marlborough Street – to go ahead. The two of them ran into the stables and I left them to rejoin the Lewis gunner.

In Marlborough Street we met a few of our lads and asked them about the Irregulars who'd escaped from Upper Sackville Street. 'We got them all,' one of the lads said, and with that knowledge my mate and I returned up Marlborough Street to Parnell Street and reported back to the shop which served as our command post. We were tired and hungry when we reported in, and our lieutenant secured meals and beds for us in a hotel nearby and I enjoyed a good night's sleep.

Cathal Brugha had not been killed outright when he was shot.

The single bullet was fired low and hit him in the thigh where it severed the femoral artery. He was rushed to the Mater Hospital by men of the St John's Ambulance Brigade, but he had lost a great deal of blood and died at the hospital on Friday morning, 7 July.

As the commander of his small garrison, Cathal Brugha should have known – and *must* have known – the ruse his men were attempting when they put on those Red Cross armlets before leaving him. But his fatal error was in assuming that anyone in the Findlater building who'd watched his men dash across the lane would not, after a while, expect any more to come out and that then he, too, could safely slip away. The flames eventually drove him out, but he had waited as long as possible until Thomas' Lane was deserted: there wasn't a soul in sight and all his men had crossed the lane without a shot being fired.

With his death, Brugha became an anti-Treatyite martyr: part of Findlater Place was subsequently renamed Cathal Brugha Street by the Dublin Corporation, and the Fianna Fáil party made him their hero.

Michael Collins was – and still is – a national hero to the great majority of the Irish people, but since Collins championed the fight for the Treaty, the anti-Treatyites needed an alternative figure to compete for the popular imagination. De Valera had to be discarded because he was too remote and devious to become a credible folk hero and there was really no one else until Dorothy Macardle in her book *The Irish Republic*[53] spelled out the legend of Cathal Brugha's death.

Her version of what happened in the smoke-filled lane behind Upper Sackville Street late that Wednesday afternoon provided the anti-Treatyite cause and the Fianna Fáil party with just the sort of material they wanted. Her picture of Brugha emerging from the flames to face the levelled rifles of the enemy host and choosing to fight it out against hopeless odds rather than surrender was intended to portray Brugha in the role of a Gaelic hero. But Cathal Brugha was no Cúchulainn, and the scene portrayed by Macardle is more Germanic than Celtic. It is unfortunate that in the absence of an authentic account of what really happened, Dorothy Macardle's version has been accepted as sacred script so that both anti-Treatyite propagandists and historians have perpetuated the legend of 'the ring of steel' and 'the one hundred levelled rifles'.

But despite Macardle, doubts lingered on even in the minds of the faithful and it is significant that as the fiftieth anniversary of Brugha's death approaches, anti-Treatyite sympathisers and Fianna Fáil supporters have made desperate efforts to revise the legend. Those efforts include the lecture on Cathal Brugha given by Major Florence O'Donoghue to the Cumann Tir Chonaill (Donegal Club) in Dublin's Royal Hibernian Hotel on Monday night, 25 April 1966, and the publication of *Cathal Brugha* by Tomás Ó Dochartaigh (Foilseacháin Náisiúnta Teo) in the autumn of 1969.

I've met three different individuals who have 'admitted' – in recent years – to having 'shot' Cathal Brugha, and I know of one odd character who'd 'confessed' to having fired the Lewis gun!

The only heroes in Findlater Place that fateful afternoon were the two Dublin fellows who wanted to save the horses in Findlater's stables from being burned to death. They weren't 'soldiers of the Republic' or 'legionaires of the Rearguard'; they were just a couple of decent Dublin workingmen.

10

On Thursday morning, 6 July – after a good night's rest – our small party of troops, who'd been in the Findlater buildings since Sunday 2 July, was sent to occupy Independent House in Middle Abbey Street and protect it from being seized by anti-Treatyites. The staff of the *Irish Independent* clearly resented our presence and did everything they could to make our stay as uncomfortable as possible. They resented us not because we were soldiers or because they were sympathetic to the anti-Treatyites; they resented us simply because we were *Irish* troops.

Today, most readers of the *Irish Independent* ('Ireland's most popular newspaper') probably don't realise how reactionary and pro-British that newspaper once was. Under the proprietorship of William Murphy it not only tried to break Larkin's and Connolly's Transport and General Workers' Union in 1913, but in 1916 its editorials called for the execution of the leaders of the Rising!

One night I decided I'd had enough of trying to sleep on the floors, tables, etc., so about midnight I left Independent House and started to walk down towards Amiens Street Station determined to find a railway compartment where I could sleep comfortably on some cushions. I didn't meet a soul until I reached Corporation Street – which was notorious for its prostitutes – when two women suddenly stepped out of a doorway and, grabbing me by the arms, pleaded for money for everything from a 'drop of the crathur' to 'bread for the childer.' I tried to tell them that I had no money, that we hadn't been paid since the fighting started, but it was no use. The two of them kept pulling at me until I reached Amiens Street where I stopped and told them they could have all the money I had.

I reached into my trousers pocket and drew out all the loose change I could find – 9½d – and offered it to them. One of the women looked at the coins closely and then suddenly hit the back of my hand throwing all the coins into the air as she cursed in Dublin's foullest language. While she continued her stream of abuse, I unslung my rifle and, placing its barrel on the top of her head, fired off a round.

With a terrible scream the woman grasped at her head: she must have had the fright of her life when she thought I'd shot off the top of her skull. Her screeches could have awakened the dead in Glasnevin Cemetery as she turned and fled down Amiens Street with her companion. As they ran, the first one stopped every now and then to feel the top of her head. They had gone half the length of the street before they stopped running, while I stood in the middle of Amiens Street splitting my sides laughing. Then, finally realising I'd made eedjits of them, they renewed cursing me at the top of their voices. This time, I knelt on one knee in the centre of the street and carefully aiming above their heads, I fired off another round. Jasus! They fled for good, then.

While I was standing there, I noticed a light burning in the doorway of the North Star Hotel just opposite the station so I walked in and got a room for the night. Once inside the room I barricaded the door with a heavy old bureau, and with my rifle in bed beside me, I slept soundly until about three o'clock in the afternoon. After a good wash and tidying up I felt like a new man, and casually tossing the room key back to the desk clerk as I left the hotel, I returned to duty at Independent House.

In mid-morning a lorry drew up outside the main entrance of Independent House and a party of fresh troops came in to relieve us. We'd been given no advance warning of their arrival, but when we were told to pick up our gear and climb aboard the lorry, we were very glad to be leaving. The lorry took us to Beggar's Bush barracks and I found myself back in the same barrack room I'd occupied when I first joined up.

During the afternoon I heard some of the lads discussing a rumour that our GHQ was about to form a special unit from selected volunteers. No one seemed to know either the purpose or the destination of the proposed new force, but it raised a lot of interest and speculation among the lads in the barracks. Everyone knew that something big was afoot; recruitment for the National Army had been stepped up in the previous week, and our original strength of about 4,000 men was increasing at the rate of several hundred men each day.

I learned from the lads in the room that a list had already been made – that same morning – of those who wished to volunteer for the new force. I also learned that because it was likely the new unit would soon leave Dublin for somewhere 'down the country,' as they say, those who'd given in their names had been allowed to go home for the rest of the day if their families lived in Dublin but that they had to be back within the barracks for a roll call after tea time.

After tea time, however, it was obvious that several of the volunteers hadn't shown up, so I decided to take advantage of whatever opportunity there might be of heading for the country with the new unit and, offering to take the place of one of the absent volunteers, fell in with the rest.

An officer came through the ranks checking our names and when he came to me he said, 'I don't see your name on this list. Why did you fall in?' I told him I was fed up with the city and rather than stay in the barracks doing nothing, I'd prefer to see the country again. He said he'd have to check and see if it was all right for me to join the group because my name wasn't on the list, but when he came back he gave me a big grin and said, 'It's all right, Seán. You can come along.'

The next morning we were ordered to fall in with our rifles and equipment. There was considerable excitement among us as we speculated as to where we might be going. We soon found out! We were told that we now formed the Dublin Guards flying column and were on our way to Nenagh (aboard a small convoy of Lancias and Crossley tenders) where we would stop and rest for the night.

Our GHQ had already begun a major offensive against the Irregular forces that controlled most of the hinterland south of a line between the cities of Limerick and Waterford. This was the area that largely comprised Dev's so-called Munster Republic in which the Irregulars – under the leadership of Liam Lynch, their Chief-of-Staff – had proclaimed at Mallow (on 30 June) their effective secession from the authority of Dáil Éireann.

After we had destroyed their headquarters in the Four Courts and captured some of their leaders (including Rory O'Connor and Liam Mellows), the leadership of the Irregular faction began to disperse. The subsequent destruction of the Sackville Street headquarters (in the Gresham and Hammam Hotels) of Oscar Traynor's contingent, and the rout at Blessington during the first few days of July of the Irregular reinforcements from the south, completed the dispersal of the faction's leadership with its survivors fleeing into the country. Liam Lynch, reassuming the position of Chief-of-Staff,[54] had been caught while trying to escape from Dublin soon after the attack on the Four Courts. Liam Tobin took Lynch to General O'Duffy (our Assistant Chief-of-Staff) who let him go free again on the understanding that Lynch would take no further part against the National Army. Liam Lynch then made his way to Mallow where, on Thursday 29 June, he set up a temporary HQ before moving on the same day to the city of Limerick where he established a more permanent headquarters. With his strongest support behind him in the counties of Kerry, Cork, and Limerick, Lynch now occupied a strong defensive position.

When attempts begun on Tuesday 11 July failed to dislodge the Irregulars from their positions in Limerick city, our GHQ announced on 13 July[55] the appointment of General Eoin O'Duffy as OC South-Western Command, and ordered additional troops into the drive against the Irregular forces in that area. Our flying column was to spearhead that drive and to strengthen and support the bulk of the force which consisted largely of raw, inexperienced soldiers. Liam Lynch, in the meantime, must have appreciated the vulnerability of his HQ because he moved it east to Clonmel on 11 July and then south to Fermoy on 15 July.

The numerical strength of the Irregulars – on paper at least – was greater than ours, and they had seized large quantities of arms and ammunition from those barracks vacated by the departing British troops. They had, with the acquiescence of the British, confiscated the cargo of military supplies aboard the British admiralty vessel *Upnor* at the end of March. Money was never any problem for the Irregulars; they simply raided a convenient bank and walked out with all the cash they could get their hands on.

But apart from the leadership of a few splendid fighters, such as Liam Lynch himself, who'd proved themselves during the Tan War against the British, the Irregular forces were only the shambles of an army. We had the insuperable advantage of being the National Army. We looked it ... and we proved it. Our leader was Mick Collins, idol of the nation, and for those of us in the Dublin Guards, at least, there was no other man in Ireland for whom we'd more gladly die.

We arrived at Nenagh tired and hungry about nine o'clock in the evening, and after a good meal we bunked down for the night in the old British army barracks while the regular garrison stood guard. Early next morning we boarded the lorries again and set out for Ballina and then on to Killaloe where we were to stay that night. The main road was frequently blocked with trees cut down by the Irregulars, and we often had to stop in order to clear a path for the vehicles in the convoy. In some places the main road was so heavily blocked that we were forced to detour through the side roads. Even these were sometimes impassable, and rather than allow ourselves to be delayed until all the trees were cleared, we had no choice but to get out of the lorries and leg it. Occasionally a shot was fired at us from across the fields and then one or two of us would chase off in the direction from which the shot came. One of our lads, a Tipperary fellow who joined us at Nenagh as a sort of guide, could run like a hare and the moment he heard a shot he'd leap over the hedge and tear off after the padjoe. He was just an ordinary country lad, but that Tipperary fellow (whose name, I believe, was Coppinger) had lots of real courage and I was glad when I heard several months later that he was promoted to the rank of lieutenant. The Irregulars, however, weren't a serious problem except for the occasional sniper; whenever they saw us coming they fled into the countryside without attempting to shoot it out. Judging from the report of their rifles, most of the snipers were armed with Mausers which had a distinctive 'snap' when fired.

It was a beautiful morning as we marched into Killaloe on the road along the banks of the River Shannon. The sun shone across the waters and over the loveliest of green hills and meadows. For a while

I didn't think the scene could be made more perfect: and then I heard the church bells ringing for morning mass. When the other lads saw how entranced I was with this peaceful scene of lovely Irish countryside, some of them teased me about it. But I didn't care, for I felt I was the High King of Ireland.

Shortly after arriving in Killaloe we were assigned to various billets in the town and I was one of a party sent to a big house that resembled a small private hotel. In the afternoon I took the opportunity of visiting the famous waterfalls because I wasn't sure of how long we'd remain in Killaloe. After tea that evening I went in search of a fellow named White who'd been a great friend of mine in Dartmoor Prison. I hadn't seen him since the time of his release until the night we pulled into Nenagh when I spotted him climbing out of a tender full of troops. We were delighted to see each other again but our reunion was short-lived because our two groups were separated for the night. We had just enough time to vow that when we got to Killaloe we'd get together once again and have a night on the town.

I roamed around the town checking the various billets in hope of finding White, but without success. Then I met one of my own crowd who'd been assigned to do guard duty that night but who begged me to stand in for him. He was a Dubliner and said he had a brother (or a cousin) living in Killaloe whom he hadn't seen in years and might not see again for a long time. I felt sorry for him and knew he'd do the same for me if I were in his situation, so I agreed. Anyway, it was too late for me to continue looking for White, although there was a possibility that I might meet him if he came through the street while I was on sentry duty.

I finished a two-hour spell of guard duty at midnight, but White never showed up and I turned in when my relief took over. It seemed as if I'd just got nicely settled down for forty winks when the sound of a shot rang out in the night. The entire picket turned out to investigate, and we soon learned that the sentry had fired at someone creeping along in the dark street. After a quick search we came across a figure huddled up on the ground close to the walls of an old house. When we turned him over to take a good look at him, we saw he'd been shot through the head. It was White. O Jesus! My heart nearly broke when I saw the poor fellow lying there dead. Everyone felt terrible about it especially when they learned he'd been with me in Dartmoor.

In the morning I got the full story of the tragedy. When we failed to find each other the previous evening, White had gone off in search of a friend of his in Killaloe and the two of them got drunk on poitín. Returning late at night and full of drink, White was shot as he was trying to find his billet by the sentry who mistook him for an infiltrator. Of course nobody could blame the sentry; any of us would have done the same thing. Our officers had warned us that we were in Irregular territory and the picket had been instructed to take no chances. The sentry couldn't have seen that White was, in fact, one of our own soldiers, because it was a very dark night and in those days none of the Irish country towns had street lighting.

From that day until this – although, God knows, I've had a thousand opportunities to do so – I've never touched a drop of poitín.

Our departure from Killaloe was delayed for a couple of days until reinforcements of additional troops and lorries joined us for the move to Limerick. When we were within two or three miles of the city, Captain Tom Flood, the OC of our flying column, called a halt to tell us that the Irregulars had been driven out of Limerick but that they might be waiting to ambush us as we advanced along the road. We then spread out across the neighbouring fields and, keeping a careful watch for signs of an ambush, we cleared the way for the main convoy driving slowly down the road behind us. As we reached the outskirts of Limerick, Tom Flood called us together and we marched through the city in regular company formation.

Although Limerick had been cleared of the Irregulars, there was considerable evidence of the fierce ten-day fight that had taken place before our arrival; some of the barricades were still on the streets, and when we went to Cruise's Hotel (our intended quarters) we found it a shambles. Some women volunteers made tea and sandwiches for us in the hotel's kitchen before we were split up and sent off to various billets. I found myself in a party billeted at the Commercial Hotel.

We stayed in Limerick for a couple of days during which I had a brief romance with a lovely local girl whose uncle owned a pub in Limerick. She wanted me to leave the army and settle down in Limerick, promising me that her uncle would give me a job as a barman in his pub. I didn't know what to do, but on Saturday evening I promised to meet her by the Treaty Stone on the following afternoon by which time I'd have made up my mind one way or another.

About five o'clock the next morning, however, our lads were called to an early breakfast and told we were setting out from Limerick in pursuit of the Irregulars. I never saw the girl again. I felt very badly about it at the time but have learned since then that almost every soldier the world over has faced a similar dilemma at one time or another.

Our company was ordered to muster outside the Commercial Hotel with our rifles, ammunition pouches and ammunition, and we marched off to one of the main streets where we found several other contingents of troops beginning to assemble. It was a misty morning with a light drizzle of rain as Tom Flood came along and divided our flying column into advance guard, main guard and rear guard, and told us we were to lead the entire force out of Limerick. Then word was passed along that a priest was coming to give us general absolution and we all knelt in the road. As the priest passed through our ranks, we stood up again and Tom gave the order for us to march forward. I was the leading man on the right side of the advance guard and in that position led the entire force out of Limerick.

As we marched out of Limerick that Sunday morning, we learned that the Irregulars who'd begun retreating from Limerick during the night of Thursday 20 July, had decided to make a determined stand at Kilmallock, a small town about twenty miles south of Limerick. Liam Lynch and the anti-Treatyites evidently appreciated the strategic importance of Kilmallock, which not only commanded the junction of several main roads radiating into their so-called Munster Republic, but which also lay directly in the path of our intended progress towards Mallow. The Irregulars planned to block our advance by creating a stronghold within a triangular area of approxi-

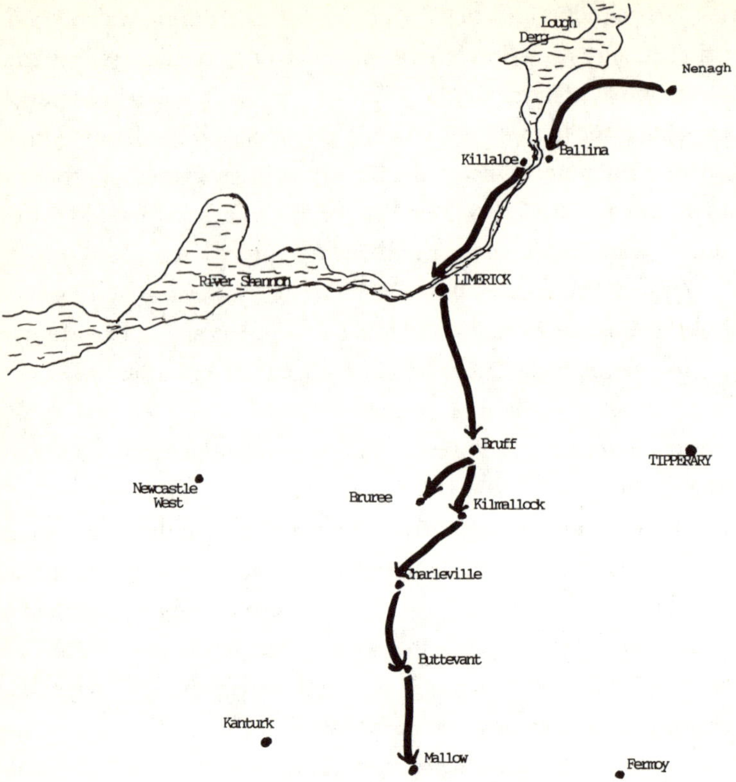

Route of Commdt Flood's Flying Column from Nenagh to Mallow (F. Maguire).

mately ten square miles bounded by the villages of Bruff in the north, Bruree in the west, and the town of Kilmallock in the south. The Dublin Guards Brigade had already established its reputation as the shock troops of the National Army – a sort of Legion of the Vanguard, one might say – and when we were chosen to spearhead the drive against the Kilmallock redoubt, we were proud of the honour.

In his book *The Civil War in Ireland*[56] Eoin Neeson includes in a chapter entitled 'The Fourteen Day Battle' an account of what he purports to be the chain of events from Sunday 23 July to Saturday 5 August, when we finally captured Kilmallock. What disturbs me most is that much of the book appears to be an eyewitness report of events experienced by Tom Flood's company during that short-lived campaign. But I was there! I was with Tom Flood all the time, and no one knows better than I that Neeson's account of our activity during those fourteen days is not what actually happened. His picture of us sloshing our way through the rain along the road from Limerick is untrue and there were only two members of our company who occupied the position of point, another lad and myself. The other fellow took left point and I was on right point. These positions were exclusively ours and we led the company all the way from Limerick to Buttevant.

With Limerick far behind us, our first contact with the Irregulars came when we were suddenly attacked by a volley of rifle fire from our right. Everyone in the column immediately dived for cover in the ditches alongside the road. Someone shouted that it was an ambush – that we were trapped and that nobody should move or we'd all be slaughtered. Luckily for me there was a huge rock about ten feet high beside me and when the firing started I took cover behind it. Looking back to where the rest of the company had taken cover, I could see that the bullets were clipping the hedges above the heads of our lads crouching in the ditches and then ricocheting in the roadway kicking up stones and spurts of dust. From my position I could see that the firing came from a stone quarry on our right and I shouted this information back to the lads.

Almost as suddenly as it had started, the firing from the quarry stopped. Our boys began to emerge cautiously from the ditches and the column resumed its advance. I took up my position on point but hadn't moved forward more than a few yards when I was startled to see a young man leap out of a hedge and land on the road in front of me. Instinctively I threw my rifle up to my shoulder and prepared to shoot him as he reached into one of his trouser pockets. I already had him in my sights and was just about to squeeze the trigger when out of the corner of my eye I saw a piece of white cloth emerge in his hand. It was a handkerchief. As he raised it above his head I lowered my rifle and ran up to him. 'You damned fool!' I yelled at him. 'You nearly got yourself killed!' But the poor lad was confused and badly frightened. I tried to explain to him that when I saw him reaching into his pocket for the white handkerchief *after* he landed on the road,

I thought he was going to draw a revolver. I searched him anyway and relieved him of a .45 calibre short service Webley and holster, a hand grenade, and a pouch of .45 calibre bullets.

Tom Flood told me to take the young prisoner to another captain a couple of hundred yards or so further back, and as I did so I saw for the first time the main body of the National Army force that was following us. Some of the men were marching, while others were travelling in lorries, and on top of one of the lorries was a newsman operating a movie camera fixed to a tripod. As I escorted my prisoner past the news photographer he swung his camera in our direction, and I remember thinking at the time that I'd be in a news reel.

I eventually handed over my prisoner – a well-groomed, fair-haired young fellow my own age – to a captain who complimented me on the capture. We noticed that there were three notches on the butt of the prisoner's revolver, but someone said that the lad (a Corkonian) had been active against the Black and Tans and that the notches probably dated from the Tan War. The No. 5 Mills bomb had a piece of string wrapped around the lever to prevent it from exploding even if the firing pin was removed, and I said it was unlikely that the lad planned to use it. I cut the string off and kept the grenade myself.

The road we marched along passed through a lovely, peaceful looking countryside of small farms and low-lying hills. In the distance we could see Knocksouna Hill where the Irregulars were reported to have gathered, and as dusk approached we left the road and advanced cautiously across a large open field before settling down for the night in a long line against some hedges.

We resumed our advance the next morning and by mid-afternoon we were crossing a large field in extended order when a machine gun suddenly opened fire on us. Ahead of the rest of the company, the two of us on point threw ourselves flat on the ground and crawled through the grass towards a ditch which lay before us. I could hear the machine gun bullets zipping into the grass about me and all I could think of was whether I would be able to get to the safety of that ditch before the machine gunner got me. Somehow I managed to avoid being hit, and when I reached the ditch I rolled into it and remained there until the firing ceased. Then I saw my mate on left point coming towards me from the other side of the field and we agreed it was then safe enough for us to return to the rest of the company.

Our company remained in those fields for the next four days while Tom Flood, who'd been given command of field operations in the area, established his headquarters in a farmhouse half a mile to the rear. I remember how glad we were of the big breakfasts and mugs of hot tea which we got in that farmhouse having lain out all night in the damp grass.

At night time we positioned pickets along the hedges and ditches to guard against a sneak attack. One night we nearly shot a fellow whom we heard whistling as he crossed the fields in the darkness; we thought he was an Irregular on night patrol scouting our positions. When we recognised the same whistling the next morning from a young boy going out to milk some cows, he told us he'd been whistling in the dark in order to avoid being mistaken for one of the Irregulars.

Our flying column resumed its advance on Saturday 29 July, but instead of launching an attack on Kilmallock, we marched to the village of Bruff which we found to be safely in the hands of our own forces. We spent that night comfortably billeted in some of the houses in the village before setting out on Sunday morning for Bruree. About fifteen of us formed an advance guard while the rest of the flying column was to follow us later in the day.

Our advance party had gone only two miles down the road towards Bruree when we were attacked by intensive firing from both sides of the road. We returned their fire, of course, but instead of allowing ourselves to be pinned down on the roadway, we took to the fields and pressed on in the direction of Bruree. We exchanged shots with the Irregulars all the way to Bruree, where we found that they were determined to make us fight for the village, too. We continued shooting it out with them until suddenly their firing ceased and we realised that the Irregulars had fled. Luckily we had suffered no casualties, and with the village securely under our control, we returned to its centre where we sat down to await the arrival of the rest of the company.

When our company sergeant major finally appeared with the remainder of our flying column, he was furious to find us looking so much at ease. Coming by a different road, the main body of the company had run into fierce opposition at a bridge and had to send back to Bruff for a field gun – an 18-pounder – before they could overcome the Irregulars. They didn't have the field gun with them when they entered Bruree; it had to be returned to Bruff immediately after they were finished with it.

It was at Bruree, however, that the worst fighting of the Kilmallock offensive was to take place, and it was there that our company suffered its worst casualties when the Irregulars launched their counterattack on Wednesday 2 August.

Prior to the fighting, which lasted about three days, Tom Flood had established his headquarters in a large country house, Bruree Lodge – a fine-looking place fit for a lord. Tom divided the company into three sections; he kept one section (to which I belonged) with him in the lodge, and sent the other two sections to man a couple of outposts on the approaches to Bruree.

One of the sections, under the command of our company sergeant major, occupied a schoolhouse and a sentry was posted to guard a bridge leading up to the schoolhouse. When an armoured car approached the bridge the sentry assumed it to be one of ours, not imagining for a moment that the Irregulars were so well equipped. Taken unawares, the sentry was immediately made a prisoner and the armoured car drove straight up to the schoolhouse, put a machine gun through one of its windows and forced the entire section – almost half our company – to surrender.

The armoured car then attacked the second outpost (a hotel building under the command of Captain Jackie Byrne), but our Lewis gunner – another big Tipperary fellow – opened up on the Irregulars from our position and the lads were able to escape from the rear of the hotel.

Those of us inside the country house with Tom Flood felt badly when we learned that our sergeant major and his section had been captured. The sergeant major was very popular with all of us and it was a severe blow to lose him. But when our Lewis gunner beat off the attack on the second outpost, we prepared for the inevitable attack on our own position. We expected that the brunt of the attack would be launched on the front of the house and we immediately barricaded the doors with as much furniture as we could find. Our big Lewis gunner mounted his machine gun behind the barricades in case the attackers tried to burst in through the front entrance.

The attackers closed in on the house and we realised we were surrounded, cut off from any possible escape. At first, Irregular snipers tried unsuccessfully to pick us off by firing through the windows. Then they fired grenades at the house. But it wasn't until we were attacked by mortar bombs that we became really worried. We never suspected that the Irregulars possessed a mortar until the shells began to land around us. Fortunately we were able to hold off the Irregulars so that they weren't able to get close enough to land any direct hits on the building, but the grounds in front of the house became pockmarked with crater holes. If the Irregulars had been able to get us within range of their grenade and mortar fire we would have been finished. There was little else we could do but accept the fact that we were under siege, hold out as long as we were able and hope that relief would come from the main force of National Army troops coming from Kilmallock. We were running short of ammunition and had to ration our dwindling supply of food.

In mid-afternoon on the second day of the siege, the firing from the Irregulars gradually died down and we thought they were withdrawing at the approach of a column sent to relieve us. After the firing had ceased for a while, most of us were glad of the opportunity to venture outside for fresh air and a chance to stretch our legs. Some of the lads wandered off in the direction of the River Maigue to take a look at a small houseboat or cabin cruiser tied up at the riverbank, while another fellow and I remained behind to examine the craters which had pitted the grounds of the lodge. All of a sudden the sound of rifle fire broke out and the lads who'd gone to take a look at the

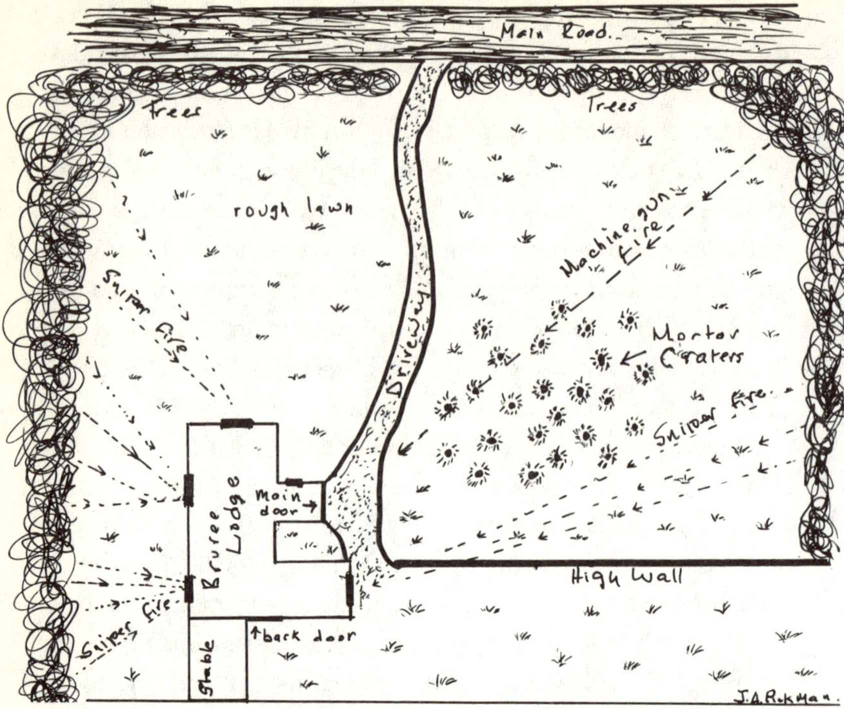

The attack on Bruree Lodge (J. A. Pinkman).

boat came running back to the lodge.

Instead of racing back to the lodge, I made the mistake of diving for cover behind some stones in a rock garden. I knew I'd been caught out in the open, but didn't realise how precarious my position really was until a machine gunner spotted me and his bullets soon began to shatter the rocks in front of me. Jasus! I cursed myself for being caught in such a tight spot and for not having my rifle. I knew that sooner or later a burst from the machine gunner would get me if I remained where I was, but that if I tried to run back to the lodge I risked being picked off before I got inside the building. The house wasn't all that far away but its front door was heavily barricaded and I could imagine myself being riddled as I struggled to open the door. From where I lay I could see the house quite clearly and as I was debating the risk of making a dash for it, I noticed that an arched window – like the sort one might see in a church – on the side of the front porch had been left ajar. It was my only chance so I ran for it and leapt high enough to go crashing through the glass, landing on top of the barricade piled in front of the door. As I went through the window, my cap – thank God! – flew off and skimmed through the air ahead of me. 'It's Seán!' the lads shouted as they saw the cap, and they ran forward to pick me out of the furniture. Our Lewis gunner had gone as white as death. 'I thought it was one of the padjoes,' he said. 'I had my finger on the trigger ...'

Luckily I hadn't been cut by the glass, and when I got over the shock of it all I took up a firing position at one of the windows as the Irregulars resumed the attack. I hadn't bothered to retrieve my cap which lay somewhere among the entangled furniture of the barricade and remained bareheaded during the remainder of the attack. When the Irregulars finally broke off the engagement and withdrew, I discovered that my mop of hair was full of glass splinters. The lads warned me not to try to comb out the splinters, saying that they'd eventually fall out on their own, and for several days I couldn't even wear the cap that had saved my life.

Our worst moments came on the final day of the siege when the Irregulars drove an improvised armoured car to within six feet of the front door of the lodge. During a furious exchange of fire, the rear doors of the armoured vehicle flew open and some of its occupants made a reckless attempt to storm the lodge. The intensity of our firing drove all of them back to the vehicle except one who was left badly injured on the ground. When a comrade returned to pick him up one of our lads at the window cried, 'An act of mercy!' and we all ceased firing until the wounded man was back inside the armoured car.

We then expected the vehicle to retire completely from the fray but were surprised to see it halt only a short distance from the lodge and return for two more desperate assaults. But the vehicle was being driven in such an increasingly erratic manner that we concentrated our fire on its more vulnerable parts – including the gaps in its armoured plating – in an effort to disable it totally. I don't know if we did more injury to the car than to its crew, but after the third assault the vehicle lumbered off and then careened wildly down the road and out of sight.

When our supplies of food and ammunition were getting so low that we couldn't have held out much longer, the Irregulars stopped their attack. We were trying to imagine why they had ceased firing, when we saw an advance party of General Murphy's troops approaching to relieve us. Most of the Irregulars managed to escape; those who were captured surrendered their rifles and were led off down the road.

General W. R. E. Murphy (an ex-lieutenant colonel of the British army), who had been given command of the forces in Kilmallock, himself arrived soon afterwards in a bus and congratulated us on holding out against the Irregulars. He asked me my name and then asked me how I liked the new web equipment which had been issued to us in Limerick. I was frank with him and told him that I didn't like it. When he asked me why, I told him that I preferred the old cross straps with the leather ammunition pouches and said that the new webbing was too much like a harness.

'It's the best there is,' he said. 'I think you'll like the webbing once you get used to it.' Then he slapped me on the shoulder and moved on.

What was left of our company piled aboard the charabanc and we were driven back to Limerick *via* Bruff. We were famished by the time we reached Limerick where we were given a huge meal and assigned to comfortable billets for the night. A day or so later we climbed aboard the charabanc and were driven to Bruff from where we marched to Kilmallock. Kilmallock, however, was already in the hands of the National Army. General Murphy had launched his attack on Kilmallock at dawn on Saturday 5 August, and his troops swept into the town with surprisingly little resistance. The Irregulars had chosen to abandon the place and were reported to be retreating southwards in the direction of Charleville (now known as Rath Luirc) and Buttevant.

General Murphy garrisoned Kilmallock with a contingent of his own forces and we marched off towards Charleville without incident only to find that the Irregulars had left for Buttevant when they learned of our approach. It was too late that day for us to carry on for Buttevant, so we billeted for the night in a house on the main street of Charleville. Most of the people in Charleville avoided us like the plague, and because we thought they were sympathetic to the Irregulars, we posted a sentry on the door and slept with our rifles by our sides.

The next morning we all went to mass and communion. Then we noticed a change in the people's attitude towards us. Until they saw us go to mass and communion, they had believed the Irregulars' propaganda that we were all recruited from the Black and Tans!

After mass the woman of the house cooked us a big breakfast of bacon and eggs which she served up with plates of freshly baked soda bread and mugs of hot, sweet tea. I'll always remember how grateful we were to that wonderful woman, but when we were leaving and tried to thank her for her hospitality, she wouldn't hear of it. Instead, she shook hands with each of us and said how proud she was to be able to cook a meal for Irish soldiers in Irish uniform. It was reassuring for us who were fighting a civil war to know that the ordinary, decent people whom we met in the country were proud of us and supported us.

After a party of General Murphy's troops arrived to garrison Charleville, we set off for Buttevant. My mate and I took up our positions on point, and the company marched in extended order along both sides of the road. One of our lads had a melodeon and he struck up a tune as he walked in the centre of the road beside our big Lewis gunner. Ah, Jasus! There wasn't a happier bunch of fellows in all Ireland as we marched in the sunshine together along the road to Buttevant that morning.

Suddenly the reports of scattered shots rang out from the direction of a bridge ahead of us and everyone except the Lewis gunner scattered for cover. The big Tipperary lad, who carried the Lewis gun on his shoulder everywhere he went, ran up the road firing off a drum of ammunition in the direction of the bridge. Then a dispatch rider who'd been trailing behind us on his motorcycle roared past and headed for the bridge. Steering the bike with one hand while he held a revolver in the other, the dispatch rider disappeared over the bridge, blazing away at the padjoes. 'He's a madman!' someone shouted, and none of us expected to see the rider come back alive. But the firing stopped and after a few silent, anxious moments the sound of the motorcycle returning assured us that the dispatch rider hadn't been killed.

'Don't ever do a thing like that again!' Tom Flood roared at him when the rider returned grinning. 'Don't you ever do a crazy thing like that again!' But despite Tom's outburst we all admired the dispatch rider's courage.

We resumed the advance – more cautiously this time – answering the sporadic shots fired at us until eventually we came to a priest's house in a wooded area not far from the road. The priest's housekeeper was standing on the doorstep and despite the ricocheting bullets flying against the slate roof, insisted we come in for some tea. All we wanted was a little refreshment before carrying on for Buttevant with the least delay, but the parish priest didn't want to let us go. 'Ah, stay for a while!' he said. 'I've been waiting all these years to see the sight of our own young men in Irish uniform.' But Tom Flood was impatient for us to be on our way, especially when we heard the sound of sporadic rifle fire getting closer.

'For Jasus' sake, let us go!' said Tom, while we were laughing at his predicament. 'We've got to get to Buttevant.'

When we finally got to Buttevant, we headed straight for the British-built military barracks, only to find it had been reduced to an enormous heap of rubble. The buildings had been dynamited by the Irregulars in order to prevent us from using them, but we were disgusted at the sheer wantonness of the destruction. So much sabotage had already been inflicted by the Black and Tans that we couldn't understand how even the most bitter of the anti-Treatyites could continue to do the same sort of thing.

Tom decided we should search the buildings, and dividing the company into two sections – each of which was to enter the barracks from opposite sides – told us to meet in the centre. He warned us to be on the look-out for snipers and booby-traps, and we picked our way carefully through the piles of stones and slates beneath the shattered walls. Luckily for us there were neither mines nor snipers about the place, and after a quick search of the town itself, we learned that the Irregulars had already fled towards Mallow, a larger town about eight miles further south.

We remained in Buttevant that night but the next day we got word that the townspeople of Mallow were waiting anxiously for our arrival. The Irregulars who'd been fleeing before us had reached Mallow where they'd blown up its famous ten-arch bridge. The people of Mallow were afraid that their only other bridge across the River Blackwater would be similarly destroyed. We were told that the town's two leading clergymen – a Catholic and a Protestant – had, in a rare ecumenical gesture for that time, led their congregations in prayers on the bridge defying the Irregulars to blow it up.

We got ready to set out for Mallow, but just as I was about to take up my usual position on right point, Tom Flood asked me to remain behind in Buttevant with a small section of the company.

'Tom,' I said, 'I've been at the head of the company all the way from Limerick and I'd like to lead the column into Mallow.'

'Listen, Seán!' he said. 'We've got to leave a few of the lads behind ... if we don't, the padjoes might slip back again ... Captain Jackie Byrne is staying behind and he's asked especially for you ... I want you to stay for his sake and mine ...' Both Tom Flood and Jackie Byrne knew I wanted to go on to Mallow with the rest of the company, but they also knew that I would give the Irregulars a good run for their money if any of them should return to Buttevant.

As the company marched off they wished us good luck because they didn't expect to see us again. Most of us had been together since we left Beggar's Bush barracks for Nenagh, and many of us had been comrades since before the Kilkenny fight. It was always a sad moment whenever some of the lads were separated from the company, and when my mate on left point offered to stay behind so I could lead the boys into Mallow, it showed the sort of comradeship that existed among us.

The company disappeared down the road and Captain Byrne assigned us to our posts. We missed the boys and were feeling pretty lonesome when a couple of girls emerged from a row of little houses near the barracks and came over to chat with us. They seemed very friendly and when they asked us for a couple of cigarettes we gladly gave them a few. But the parish priest came along and when he saw the girls smoking with us he got into a terrible rage and chased the poor girls back to the village. We roared with laughter at the sight of the priest chasing the girls and giving them hell as they fled, but some of the townspeople who'd been watching the incident told us afterwards that the girls had been the tarts of the British garrison stationed in Buttevant. When we arrived the girls had evidently hoped to establish themselves in our favour, but when we learned what they were, we'd have nothing to do with them. It had apparently been a custom for the British army to accommodate such girls in houses close to the military barracks in country towns across Ireland. Despised by the local townsfolk and shunned by us, the lot of such girls was a wretched one.

The people of Buttevant were very good to us and invited us into their homes, but by the third day I was so bored with guarding a ruined barracks that when a Crossley tender arrived from Mallow with supplies, I couldn't resist the temptation to hop aboard the tender and return with it to Mallow. Tom Flood was the first to meet me when the tender reached Mallow and he roared with laughter when he saw me. 'I knew you wouldn't stay in Buttevant,' he said. 'I knew you'd be down here ... I knew it! But wait until Jackie Byrne hears about it! He'll come down and have you shot!'

Captain Byrne was furious when he heard I'd gone to Mallow but when he eventually caught up with me he admitted he wasn't too surprised that I'd left Buttevant. He knew I'd been with the company all the way from Dublin and said he understood how I felt. I told him that it wasn't as if I'd let him down; if we had thought there was going to be any trouble in Buttevant, I would have stayed on. I could see he was still annoyed with my leaving Buttevant without his permission, but as time went on he became one of the best friends I ever had.

(After my release from the army I happened to meet Jackie Byrne outside a shop in Dublin. We were delighted to see each other again and celebrated our reunion by going into a nearby cafe to talk about old times over a cup of tea. Jackie insisted I go home with him to meet his family, but when he introduced me to his mother I recognised her immediately as the same woman who, in the early days of the Civil War, had handed me the envelope outside Amiens Street Station to give to Captain Paddy Daly. She recognised me, too, but neither of us let on that we'd ever met before; we just nodded knowingly to each other.)

One weekend in Mallow the Irish Army Pipers Band arrived from Dublin and we all turned out to meet them. One of the pipers was Jimmy Lowe, Paddy Lowe's brother. We were so surprised to see each other that we hardly knew what to say. Jimmy seemed to be just as embarrassed as I was until we finally shook hands and I blurted out that I hadn't expected to meet him because I'd heard he'd joined the Irregulars. Then Jimmy started to grin sheepishly and said that he'd been told *I* had deserted to the Irregulars, and we soon found ourselves laughing as we explained to each other how we'd been misled.

I told him that before the fighting began at the Four Courts I'd often been stopped in Gardiner Street by some of the anti-Treatyites who told me that I was about the only one of the Liverpool Volunteers who hadn't joined their crowd in the Four Courts. They mentioned the names of a few fellows – including Jimmy Lowe – whom I'd known in Liverpool, and although most of them had been either inactive or were Trucers, I did feel badly when I was told my former comrades in Liverpool expected me to join them. 'Bring your rifle,' they said, 'and join your comrades in the fight against the Free State.' Some of the Liverpool crowd had deserted from the National Army and, taking their rifles with them, had joined the Four Courts garrison. But I couldn't do it and had no use for an outfit that would accept such men.

Then Jimmy Lowe said he'd been told much the same story; that he'd heard that *he* was almost the last of the Liverpool company who hadn't joined the Four Courts garrison.

11

THE SOLID LIMESTONE WALLS OF THE Mallow creamery provided us with a ready-made fortress, and our company was billeted in the large store-room attached to it. After I'd stowed my gear there, I got myself cleaned up and went into town to enjoy the luxury of a shave in a barbershop. The few idlers sitting around the shop quietened their banter when I entered, but the barber greeted me warmly, and ushering me into a chair, draped a linen sheet around me. He lathered my face, stropped the razor, and carried on the usual barber's discourse about the weather and the state of the crops as he began to shave me. Then, after the first few deft strokes, I suddenly felt his free hand tighten its grasp on my head as he raised his voice. 'Wouldn't it be a shocking thing if I made a slip and cut the throat of a Free State soldier?' he asked sarcastically.

The barber paused for a moment, holding the razor a few inches from my throat as he glanced towards his audience sitting on the benches around the walls. The idlers roared, thoroughly enjoying my predicament as I lay back helplessly in the chair with my neck exposed to the razor. Sure of his audience, the barber resumed the shaving, but with every other stroke he reminded me of how close I was to having my throat cut. Some of the fellows around the walls took the opportunity to exercise their country wit and egged on the barber with a variety of anecdotes about the killing of farm livestock.

Having taken as long as he could, the barber eventually finished shaving me without even nicking my skin. 'And how was that for a close shave?' he asked me with a sneer as he leaned over to remove the sheet from my shoulders. The eedjits around the wall began to clap, but they stopped suddenly when they saw the barber stiffen with fright. As he whipped the linen sheet away, the barber found himself staring at the barrel of the cocked .45 calibre revolver I was holding in my lap. Jasus! You never saw a room empty as fast as that barbershop! Only the barber remained. He was paralysed with fear when he realised I'd held the revolver in my lap from the moment he'd draped the linen sheet around me.

'Now tell me who had a close shave!' I said as I got up from the chair and walked out.

My narrowest escape in Mallow took place only a day or so later when someone hurled a grenade at me as I was walking towards the bridge across the Blackwater. But the thrower's aim was off, and the grenade landed in the road a few yards ahead of me. As I dived for shelter into the nearest doorway, the grenade rolled towards the gutter where it finally came to rest, and I crouched in the doorway waiting for the damned thing to explode. The road was deserted at the time except for three or four youngsters who, having seen the grenade roll to a stop in the gutter and fail to explode, began to move towards it. I yelled at them to stay back but their curiosity was so keen they merely paused before edging closer to the grenade. As the seconds passed and the grenade failed to explode, I concluded it was a dud and got up from my crouching position. Then I saw why the grenade – a No. 5 Mills bomb – had failed to go off: the pin retaining the detonator hadn't been fully extracted. One of the lugs holding the pin was bent, and whoever threw the grenade hadn't been able to pull the pin free of both lugs. This probably accounted for the erratic aim of the thrower who likely panicked when he couldn't get the pin free and then got rid of the grenade in a hurry.

In the meantime, my warning to the children to stay back went unheeded and fearing they might pick up the grenade, I dashed from the doorway, grabbed it up and ran for the bridge. I could feel the grenade warm in my hand and prayed frantically as I raced to the bridge to throw it into the river. My guardian angel must surely have been protecting me that day! No sooner had I thrown the grenade over the bridge than there was a muffled roar as it exploded beneath the water.

Apart from sporadic attacks either by lone snipers or by marauding bands of Irregulars, large-scale resistance to the National Army had, however, ceased by mid-August. While General Murphy's troops were advancing on Kilmallock, a contingent of the Dublin Guards under General Paddy Daly had landed at Fenit (on the Kerry coast) on 2 August and swept through Tralee and Co. Kerry, and on the night of 8 August General Emmet Dalton's force had landed at Passage West and then pressed through Cork. As the so-called 'Munster Republic' collapsed, our duties were to garrison the principal towns and mop up the scattered Irregulars and their leaders.

One evening Tom Flood called me aside after tea time and told me he wanted me to go with him on a special job that night. 'Don't let on to anyone else,' he said. 'Just have your rifle and ammunition and be at the field gate behind the creamery at ten o'clock.'

When I turned up at the gate at ten o'clock that night, I was surprised to meet another lad from the company who arrived there almost the same time that I did. He was as surprised to see me as I was to see him and said that Tom had asked him, too, to be there. Then Tom arrived and told us that he'd received information that Dev was expected at midnight at an abandoned railway station north of Mallow for a rendezvous with some of the leading Irregulars in the area. The three of us set off immediately, but to avoid meeting anyone else we cut across the fields parallel to the road, ducking low behind the hedges whenever we heard footsteps on the roadway.

Eventually we reached the platform of a small, disused station north of Mallow (on the Great Southern and Western Railway line leading to New Twopothouse Village) close to the Union Work House, and soon realised that it was an ideal location for a clandestine meeting.

Tom said very little because, I suppose, he was so greatly aware of the awful responsibility he shouldered. We didn't plan to make De Valera a prisoner; we intended to shoot him if we got the chance to do so – that was why Tom had chosen us. He knew he could depend on us. Personally, I had no qualms about shooting Dev whom I believed was so largely responsible not only for the outbreak of the Civil War, but also for its prolongation.

Tom posted the other volunteer and me to each of the two entrances to the station while he drew his revolver and lay down on the platform so as to be able to get De Valera if he came along the railway track. My comrade and I lay in the grass beneath the hedges close to the station's entrances. Making sure my magazine was full, I slipped a round into the breech of my rifle and moved the safety catch into the 'off' position. I'm sure the other volunteer did the same. Midnight came but neither Dev nor anyone else showed up, and although the three of us – each with a bullet 'up the spout' – remained carefully hidden for the next few hours, there was no sign of visitors. Then, at the first light of dawn, Tom called out telling us we could get up. Disappointed that we didn't get a chance at Dev we headed back to Mallow. We didn't meet anyone on the way nor did we let on to the rest of our comrades about the attempted ambush.

A few nights later Tom Flood detailed a small party of us to accompany him on a search for the leaders of a North Cork Brigade of Irregulars. He told us that he'd been tipped off that they were hiding in the deserted home of an ex-British army officer a few miles outside Mallow.

As we approached the house – a fine mansion typical of the sort that ex-British army officers liked to purchase in Ireland when they retired – Tom divided our party into two groups, one of which was to enter the front of the house while the other was to enter through the rear. He warned us to be very careful, as the lads inside the house might want to make a fight for it.

No one answered the front door when Tom knocked, so we forced our way in and began to search the place. I was sent to search the bedrooms upstairs, and coming to a room that was locked, I knocked on the door.

'Don't come in!' shouted a woman's voice from inside the bedroom. I told her that I wouldn't enter until she had time to get dressed, but she kept up a steady stream of abuse calling me a 'Green and Tan' and telling me I had no right to call myself an Irishman.

After I had given her enough time to dress, I knocked on the door again but she refused to open it so I butted it open with my rifle. The young woman inside the room renewed her abuse the moment I entered the bedroom, but fell silent when I noticed a few cigarette butts scattered on the floor beside the bed.

'Is the bed still warm?' I asked her as I slid my hand between the sheets. The bed *was* still warm and when I looked at her again she was standing by the door, pale as death.

'If you open your mouth to me again,' I told her, 'I'll tell everyone downstairs that you've had a fellow in bed with you. Now,' I said, 'not another word out of you.' At that moment I felt sorry for her and didn't want to shame her in front of the others down below. There were no more insults from her and I kept my word.

As I went downstairs alone I heard one of our lads shout, 'Got them! They're in the kitchen!' We all dashed straight for the kitchen where there were three or four Irregulars with their arms raised in surrender. Three of them were the senior officers of the North Cork Brigade we were looking for and included Richard ('Dick') Bolster and John ('Jack') Willis – both of whom earned reputations for their exploits during the Tan War when they served under Liam Lynch, OC Cork No. 2 Brigade.[57] Dick Bolster's sister, an attractive blonde, regularly passed our sentry post on the surviving bridge across the Blackwater and we assumed she reported our dispositions to the Irregulars.

While two of our lads kept them covered with their rifles, the rest of us searched the kitchen thoroughly, but all we could find was a revolver in one of the drawers of a heavy, old-fashioned sideboard. One of the Irregulars then began to curse us until I went up to him and told him I'd knock his head off if he didn't shut up. Then I searched him and drew out from his pockets several rolls of bank notes. We called for Tom Flood who told us to pile the bank notes on top of the kitchen table. The fellow from whom I'd taken the notes insisted that it was his money and said I'd no right to take it from him.

'You bloody thief!' I said to him. 'You must have robbed a bank or a post office to get all this money. Is this how you're fighting for Ireland, by robbing its banks? When we fought for Ireland we didn't get a penny. And we're still broke. We haven't been paid for weeks!'

Tom told us to tie the prisoners' hands and to hang on to them with a length of rope so as not to lose them in the night, as it was pitch dark when we started back to Mallow. At first we felt sorry for the prisoners as we made our way across ploughed fields and through hedges, especially when the poor devils stumbled into ditches and got covered with mud, but we daren't untie them because they would have been off in a flash and we'd never have been able to recapture them. With the first light of dawn we were able to see each other more clearly and we had to laugh at the comical sight we made, as we hung on to the prisoners who by that time were covered from head to toe with a mixture of cow dung, mud and grass. We didn't look much better ourselves; our uniforms were splattered with the same muck as the prisoners'.

When we finally arrived back in Mallow in the early morning, the townspeople watched us from the doors and windows of their homes as we advanced in extended order through the town, with the prisoners walking in the middle of the road. When we reached the centre of the town we untied our prisoners and took them to the hotel (the Royal Hotel, I believe) which served as our HQ.

Immediately inside the hotel's front door were two rooms, one on each side of the entrance hall. One of the rooms was used as a guardroom and it was there that we left our prisoners before we returned to our quarters at the creamery. We were very tired after the night's search and the long hike back to Mallow, and after a big breakfast we all had a few hours sleep.

That evening some of us went to visit in the town but when we checked into the guardroom about nine o'clock to report our return, we heard the most terrible screams coming from the room opposite. From the shouts and cries we heard it was obvious that someone in that room was getting an awful beating. We asked a sentry at the door what was going on but all he would say was that the screams were becoming unbearable. Someone opened the door of the room and we saw the three Irregular leaders we had captured sitting at a table with sheets of paper in front of them. Behind the prisoners was an officer beating them with the butt of his revolver.

'Oh, my God!' I said. 'We didn't fight for this!' The door was quickly closed but we'd seen enough. 'That's got to be stopped. Is this what we're fighting for?' I asked the lads who were with me.

'By Jesus, no!' they said

'We could expect this from the Black and Tans,' someone said, 'but not from one of our own. This finishes the army for me.'

The guardroom was unable to tell us of Commandant Flood's whereabouts, so we searched the hotel but didn't find him there.

When we reached our quarters in the creamery, we told the rest of the lads what we'd seen being done to the prisoners we'd brought back to Mallow. Those of us who'd been in British prisons were particularly angered because we knew how unspeakably cruel it was to beat and torture helpless prisoners. We believed that if it was necessary to do so, a man should be shot, but in no circumstances should he be tortured. The lads became so incensed at what we told them that several of them suggested we should leave the army as a unit in protest against the treatment of our prisoners.

I warned them, however, not to appoint me as their leader, reminding them that I'd taken on that role during our strike in Kilkenny. We finally decided that each man in the company would act on his own; we'd leave our rifles and uniforms behind us, even though someone pointed out that we might get shot as we made our way back to Dublin.

But before we had made any irrevocable move, somebody came in and announced that Tom Flood was back at the hotel again. I got off my bed and said I was going to find Tom and tell him what I'd seen being done to our prisoners, and that I was leaving the army. I thought I owed it to Tom to at least tell him to his face why I was leaving.

When I found Tom he was sitting alone in his room and I told him straight that I was leaving the National Army and why I was doing so. I reminded him of what had happened to his own brother Frank[58] who'd been captured by the Black and Tans.

'Listen, Seán,' he said, plainly disturbed by what I'd told him. 'I did not know about what was happening to those poor fellows and it wouldn't have happened had I been here. But it did happen and I'm going to put a stop to it. The man responsible wasn't an officer from our own crowd ... he's a fellow who arrived here only recently. His name is Fitzmaurice ... James Fitzmaurice.'

Major James C. Fitzmaurice, an ex-officer of the British Royal Flying Corps who'd joined the Irish National Army after the Civil War broke out, flew a small plane on reconnaissance missions trying to locate columns of Irregulars. He was reputed to be an excellent aviator, but a few days earlier had been forced to make an emergency landing in a field about half a mile or so outside Mallow and another soldier and I were sent to guard the aircraft until a maintenance crew from Fermoy came to dismantle the plane and take it away in a lorry.

Guarding Fitzmaurice's plane was a dangerous and thankless job because the machine was such a tempting target for the Irregulars. My mate and I debated whether or not to take cover in a ditch, but we eventually decided to lie in the grass beneath the aeroplane's wings so that we could spot anyone approaching across the field.

When Tom Flood told me that it was Fitzmaurice who had been responsible for pistol-whipping the prisoners, I told Tom that Fitzmaurice deserved to be shot. 'Leave it to me,' said Tom. 'Give me twenty-four hours and I'll see that he's taken away from here. Will you give me twenty-four hours?'

'Certainly, Tom,' I said. 'But if he's still here after that I'll shoot the bastard myself.'

'If he's not out of here in twenty-four hours, he's yours,' said Tom.

I returned to tell the lads that Fitzmaurice was the officer responsible for beating the prisoners, and that Tom Flood had told me he'd be mine if he was still in Mallow after twenty-four hours.

After breakfast the following morning we learned that Fitzmaurice had already left Mallow and that was the last we saw of him. But a few years later Fitzmaurice made international headlines when on 12 April, 1928 he flew from Baldonnel Aerodrome (now known as Casement Airfield) with two Germans, Captain Hermann Kohl (co-pilot) and Baron G.V. von Huenefeld, aboard the *Bremen* – a single engine Junkers – to complete the first east-west flight across the Atlantic. For his part in the feat, Fitzmaurice (who was then a commandant and OC the Irish Air Corps) was rewarded by being promoted to the rank of colonel.[59]

Despite the Fitzmaurice incident, the episode in the barbershop, and the close call I had on the bridge when some fool threw a grenade at me, my memories of Mallow are pleasant ones. The townspeople soon learned we weren't the ogres that the Irregulars reported us to be, and relations between the people of Mallow and ourselves became increasingly cordial. We were frequently invited into people's homes and most of us, in fact, had the time of our lives while we stayed in Mallow. I shall never forget, for example, the many enjoyable evenings I spent with two brothers who owned a small shop there. One of them played the violin while the other played the accordion, and when they heard that I liked to sing, I was continually being invited to their house. Whenever I arrived, the brothers promptly closed up the shop and we then spent half the night singing and playing all the old Irish songs.

One of my closest friends in Mallow was John O'Connell, a porter at the local hospital a mile or so outside the town, and the authority upon whom Rex Taylor so largely relied for the account of the Beal na mBláth ambush (where Collins was killed) in Chapter Nineteen of his book *Michael Collins*.[60] John was not a native of Mallow – he was a Corkonian – but he knew the countryside around Mallow like the back of his hand and when Tom Flood needed a reliable guide whose integrity he could trust, he inducted John into the National Army and gave him a uniform.

Almost immediately John and I became the best of friends. Unlike most of the rest of the company, neither of us was a Dubliner and when some of the others jeered at his Cork accent I made them stop it. 'Aroo from Corrick I am aroo?' they'd say to him mimicking a Corkman's characteristic way of saying 'Are you from Cork? I am ... are you?'

During the Tan War, a party of Black and Tans made John hoist the Union Jack over Mallow Hospital and he was often tormented on that account by those of the company who didn't realise that John – who hated the Tans as much as anyone else – had hoisted the flag only because a pistol was being held to his head.

As a result of our friendship, John often invited me to accompany him on his visits to the Mallow Hospital where he introduced me to several of the nurses, one of whom I really liked. Many a pleasant evening I spent in her sitting-room which I remember so well because over the door she had placed a sign which read 'Arcadia'. In those days a nurse could have been dismissed from the hospital for having a tryst in her sitting-room, but neither John nor the other nurses ever let on and our romance was kept secret.

But what cemented the bond of friendship between John and me was our being selected to accompany Tom Flood whenever our commandant went driving through the countryside around Mallow. Tom always took John as his guide and me as his bodyguard. Not once, however, did we encounter a blocked or mined road or a blown bridge as we drove along the roads radiating from Mallow. If (as Calton Younger claims)[61] the area was 'Republican territory', we saw no evidence of 'Republican' activity! Almost every week Tom Flood – sometimes driving a Lancia armoured car but more usually a Crossley open tender – made the journey from Mallow to Limerick (where we stayed for an hour or so) and back again. John O'Connell and I always accompanied Tom on those trips and not a single shot was ever fired at us.

John O'Connell's greatest responsibility came on Sunday afternoon, 20 August 1922, when Michael Collins (our Commander-in-Chief) arrived in Mallow on his way to Cork from Dublin via Limerick.

By that time concerted opposition to the National Army had ceased and Collins wanted not only to inspect the army garrisons throughout Munster, but also to see for himself conditions in that part of the country where the fiercest fighting of the Civil War had taken place. But Collins, still grieving the loss of Arthur Griffith who had died of a stroke on 12 August, had an additional purpose in mind when he ventured forth from Dublin on a mission that was ultimately destined to take him to his beloved West Cork and, ironically, to his death.

Although still not generally acknowledged, Collins' real purpose on the mission was to personally contact some of the dissident anti-

Treatyite leaders still at large in West Cork and to effect a reconciliation with them. Anticipating the bitterness that would endure in the hearts of anti-Treatyite commanders after their forces had been defeated in the field, Collins wanted to parley with those leaders in a direct attempt to staunch the bitterness that threatened to poison the soul of the nation for the next generation. To achieve such a reconciliation would have been Collins' supreme triumph and he could then have handed over the reins of government to others.

Terribly alone after Arthur Griffith's untimely death and oppressed with the added responsibilities that only his shoulders could bear, Michael Collins desperately wanted to tie together the fibres of a nation torn apart by the Civil War. He shared – as we all did – with the most relentless of the anti-Treatyites their ultimate goal of an Irish Ireland rid of the last vestige of British control. In order to achieve that goal, however, the rent caused by the Civil War had to be repaired before it became irreparable. He saw more clearly than most others the over-riding need to restore the devastated economy of the country, and to rebuild and modernise the army before it could renew the ancient struggle with the Saxon host. Few knew that on 27 July 1922 – less than four weeks before his death – Michael Collins was arranging to send a delegation of four National Army officers to Switzerland for the purpose of studying that country's military system with a view to re-organising the Irish army.

Collins and his escort delayed in Mallow only long enough for him to make a quick inspection of our company and to promise a delegation of the town's leading clerics – Bishop Roche and Archdeacon Corbett – that the ten-arch bridge would be repaired as soon as possible. Michael Collins and his party, who had set out from Dublin at six o'clock that morning, were beginning to tire after their hectic journey and wished to reach the city of Cork before nightfall. Seeing that Collins' party needed a guide familiar with the roads between Mallow and Cork, Commandant Flood asked John O'Connell to go along with them and John, of course, agreed.

Two days later, as dusk began to fall on the fateful evening of Tuesday 22 August, Collins and his small convoy were suddenly attacked by a party of Irregulars who opened fire on the convoy as it drove through the valley of Beal na mBláth on its way back to Cork city after a tour of West Cork. The convoy halted to return the fire, Collins himself participating in the exchange. The flurried encounter was short-lived after the initial fierce volleys ricocheted through the valley. In the falling darkness accuracy was difficult for both groups and the firing died down as the ambushers began to withdraw. Suddenly the distinct report of a single shot echoed across the roadway and Michael Collins was seen to collapse. A brief burst of renewed firing from the departing Irregulars delayed his comrades from reaching their fallen hero but when they finally reached his side our chief was beyond mortal help. He had been fatally hit by a bullet in the back of his head.

I'm convinced that Michael Collins was shot by an agent of the British Secret Service in the best traditions of that organisation which date back to Elizabethan times and include the poisoning of Red Hugh O'Donnell in Simancas – most probably by James Blake, the English secret agent there. Collins' assassin – a former Intelligence officer in the British army – had successfully infiltrated the ranks of the Volunteers and risen to a senior rank in the National Army. After Collins' death, the agent was eventually reassigned to Intelligence work in North Africa and in his later years retired to London.

Although three hundred years separated the lives of Red Hugh O'Donnell and Michael Collins, their respective roles in the national struggle against the invader were remarkably similar and their deaths equally catastrophic in the course of Irish history. Early in their lives both had been imprisoned by the British as potentially dangerous to the castle regime. Refusing to succumb, each had steeled his dedication during his incarceration and renewed the fight upon regaining freedom. Both warriors possessed the charismatic qualities of leadership needed to unite the Irish people. Contending with a ruthless foe – and also with factious elements among his own followers – each led strategically brilliant campaigns against the enemy host until he paused to renew his strength before the final onslaught. And, tragically for Ireland, each of the two leaders was cut down in his prime by an unseen hand.

Ireland paid a terrible price for the loss of both Red Hugh O'Donnell and Michael Collins. With lesser men unable to assume the splendour of their leadership, Ireland sank into periods of despondency and internecine strife after their assassinations.

The first news of Collins' death caused surprisingly little impact on our company. By that time we had become so accustomed to death and rumours of death that it was some time before we realised the implications of his death – once it had been confirmed. Many of us felt a special loyalty to our Commander-in-Chief and the knowledge of his death made us more determined than ever to pursue his ideals.

Although it was small consolation, it was with a great deal of satisfaction that we learned Erskine Childers – the unremitting anti-Treatyite propagandist – had been captured in Co. Wicklow on 10 November 1922. A middle-class Englishman by birth and breeding, Robert Erskine Childers had no tangible connections with Ireland, and the motives for his involvement in the cause of Irish nationalism had long been suspected by many in the nationalist movement. Arthur Griffith had loathed the Englishman and Michael Collins shared that dislike. One can't dismiss Childers as being just another eccentric Englishman, either because of, or despite, his education at Haileybury and Cambridge. Having gained his law tripos and BA in 1893, he served as a clerk in the House of Commons for fifteen years (1895–1910), joining the City Imperial volunteers battery of the Honourable Artillery Company in 1899, and taking time out in 1900 to serve as a trooper in the Boer War. In helping to defend the British empire against the Boers, he gained first-hand experience of the new type of warfare being waged against the empire and acquired sufficient knowledge of guerrilla warfare to enable him to write about it in Volume V of *The Times History of the War in South Africa* (1907).

His authorship of the classic spy story *The Riddle of the Sands* (published in 1903) not only showed where his true loyalties lay but also indicated an ultimate personal ambition. For no overtly credible reason he took an interest in the politics of the 'Irish Question' during the four years prior to the First World War and published *The Framework of Home Rule* in 1911. During those four years, Childers had displayed a sufficiently sympathetic interest in Irish Home Rule to enable him to win the confidence of Roger Casement when Casement went to London early in 1914 to raise money for the purchase of arms for the Irish Volunteers. Childers not only assisted in raising a loan of £1,500 from among a small clique in London, but being a yachtsman also went so far as to offer his help in transporting to Ireland the rifles and ammunition which were to be purchased in Antwerp.

The story of how the arms were transported to Ireland is now legend; of how Erskine Childers and Conor O'Brien in their respective yachts *Asgard* and *Kelpie* met in the North Sea with the Hamburg tug *Gladiator* bearing 1,500 rifles and 45,000 rounds of ammunition; of how Childers and O'Brien divided the arms supplies between them, Childers landing 900 rifles and 26,000 rounds of ammunition at Howth on 26 July 1914, while O'Brien, afraid of being intercepted, transferred his portion of the arms to the yacht of Sir Thomas Myles who landed 600 rifles and the rest of the ammunition at Kilcoole (on the Wicklow coast) on 1 August 1914.

Ostensibly the Howth gun-running was a feat even more astonishing than the Larne gun-running by the Ulster Volunteers on the night of 24 April 1914 when 25,000 rifles and 3,000,000 rounds of ammunition were landed in Ulster, because it was widely known that the success of the Larne gun-running was largely due to collusion between the unionists and their supporters in the admiralty.

But the Howth gun-running deserves a closer examination than it is generally given. The crew of Sir Thomas Myles' yacht included such unlikely Irish nationalists as Captain Hervey de Montmorency of the British army, while the crew of the *Asgard* included Brigadier-General Gordon Shepherd. I'm not at all surprised that the *Asgard* was able to sail unchallenged past the British fleet assembled at Spithead for King George V's naval review! The admiralty evidently considered Childers' talents so valuable that when the First World War broke out he was called upon – despite his 'treason' – to serve as an intelligence officer and training officer with the Royal Naval Air Service, attaining the rank of major and being rewarded with the Distinguished Service Cross.

When he resumed an active interest in Irish politics after his demobilisation in 1918, he was able to capitalise on his role in the Howth gun-running and won the confidence of the people in Wicklow to the degree that they elected him a deputy to Dáil Éireann. Siding with De Valera in the Treaty debates he voted against the motion to ratify the Treaty and threw in his lot with the anti-Treatyite faction, becoming one of its leading propagandists.

Although Erskine Childers' motives for supporting firstly Irish Home Rule and then De Valera's anti-Treaty position aroused the curiosity of many nationalistic Irishmen, the part he played in the Howth affair allayed their worst suspicions. Unfortunately so many of those who were over-awed by the drama of the gun-running episode were unaware of the most significant facts regarding the rifles and ammunition with which the Irish Volunteers were to be armed to fight the British army.

The rifles were obsolete Model 71 Mausers originally issued to the German army after the Franco-Prussian War of 1870–71. The same rifle was used by the Chinese during the Boxer Rebellion! It was a single-shot weapon weighing 9 lbs., with an overall length of 52½', and designed to chamber a black powder cartridge containing a 385-grain bullet whose calibre was 11mm (.43'). Worse yet! When the fifteen thousand rifles were examined ashore in Ireland it was found that approximately half of them were useless because of mechanical defects, and about half the forty-five thousand rounds accompanying the rifles had to be discarded because they were of the 'explosive' type whose use in warfare was prohibited as early as 1868 by the St Petersburg Declaration and again by the Hague Conferences of 1899 and 1907. Some 'bargain'! And those were the rifles and ammunition brought by an ex-trooper of the Honourable Artillery Company to equip the Irish Volunteers who, if they had any weapons training at all, had fired only .22 calibre small-bore rifles.

The highly trained British infantry, on the other hand, was equipped with the Mark III Lee-Enfield rifle which weighed less than 8 lbs. and whose overall length was only 44½'. Compared to the single shot Mauser 71, the Lee-Enfield Mark III had the fastest bolt action ever designed and its magazine could hold two five-round clips of .303 calibre bullets capable of being fired very rapidly.

The irony of it all was that each member of that coterie of dilettantes who subscribed to the £1,500 loan to purchase the rifles and ammunition – not seriously expecting to be repaid – was, in fact, fully reimbursed from Volunteer funds. The British eventually repaid Roger Casement for his efforts in securing arms for the Volunteers. They hanged him.

When Erskine Childers was captured by our forces on 10 November 1922 he had a loaded automatic pistol in his hand, and he was subsequently tried by court-martial on 17 November (1922) on a charge of possessing the pistol without proper authorisation. The court found him to be technically guilty of treason and he was executed by a firing squad at 8.00 am on 24 November in Beggar's Bush barracks, maintaining to the very end his 'love' for Ireland.

Few of our company believed he'd be executed and expected that the British government would intervene – overtly or otherwise – to spare his life. I don't know if the British authorities made any attempt to save him, but I do know that his fate was sealed from the moment of his capture. Some of the officers in the Dublin Guards – men whose wit, integrity and courage had been forged in the fight for Irish independence – felt so strongly that Childers should be shot that a party of National Army officers planned to shoot him themselves if the sentence of the court wasn't carried out. They detached themselves from their normal duties and, secreting themselves close to where Childers was lodged, they lay in wait to forestall any attempt to spirit the Englishman to safety.

12

FROM ITS HEADQUARTERS AT MALLOW our company patrolled the wide, surrounding area between Buttevant in the north and Donoughmore in the south, and from Fermoy in the east as far west as Kanturk and Millstreet. The countryside to the north and east of Mallow was peaceful, and our patrolling in that direction was a relatively casual exercise. South-west of Mallow, however, our patrols were more cautious and searching as we hunted for fugitive Irregulars reportedly foraging among the wild, rain-soaked hills. Our patrols – which consisted of small parties of men – were made on foot, and when we were fortunate we billeted overnight in a village or small town.

During one patrol – when we were billeted in Millstreet – I came down with a very severe cold as a result of our tramping over the Boggeragh Mountains in the rain, and I had to go into hospital. When I was discharged I was given seven days leave and permission to go back to Liverpool for a visit with my family, but when my leave expired my mother insisted that I remain at home for another couple of weeks until I had fully recuperated.

One evening towards the end of my 'extended' leave I was playing cards with the rest of the family, when an old pal of mine, Peter Riley, called around to invite me to a farewell party for young Pat McDermot who was making his first trip to sea as a cabin boy. I really wanted to go to the party but knew how much my mother wanted me to stay at home for a quiet evening of cards. After a bit of a struggle I reluctantly declined Peter's invitation and settled down again to the game of twenty-five which my mother loved to play.

After Riley left us, he picked up young Pat McDermott and Pat's older brother, the Oriel House plainclothes man, who was also in Liverpool at the time. The three of them eventually caught a tram up to Scotland Road and dropped in to Regan's pub for a few drinks. Unfortunately they all had a bit too much to drink and young Pat McDermott, who wasn't used to spirits, began to stagger around saying he was already seasick. Pat's older brother became increasingly annoyed with the lad's behaviour and, pulling out his .45 revolver, flourished it at Pat's head and told him to sit down. In the next instant the revolver went off and the poor young lad was shot through the head – he was only fifteen years old.

The McDermott family was desolate when they learned of the tragedy and I remember my mother leading us in the rosary in thanksgiving for my not being at the party. The plainclothes man left the Oriel House force and entered a monastery. Peter Riley never really got over the shock of it all and died himself not long afterwards.

When my leave was finally over and I returned to Dublin, I told Jimmy Lowe the sad news of young Pat McDermott's death because Jimmy knew the McDermott family. Afterwards Jimmy asked me if I'd heard what had happened to Tony Deane who'd been a good friend of mine in the Liverpool Company of the Volunteers. I hadn't seen Tony since my release from Dartmoor Prison and naturally was anxious to hear what Jimmy had to say.

Jimmy told me that on the day that his brother Paddy had been killed during the Four Courts fighting, he had met Tony Deane on the bridge near Portobello barracks. Jimmy was heartbroken over his brother's death, but didn't tell Tony about it because he wasn't sure of Tony's political sympathies on the Treaty issue. Tony was dressed in civilian clothes and Jimmy thought that if he were an anti-Treatyite and learned that Paddy had been at the Four Courts with the pro-Treaty forces, then Tony might have pulled out a revolver and shot him too. Jimmy Lowe hadn't seen Tony since before the 'split' over the Treaty and his suspicions of Tony were increased when he met Tony in civvies so near Portobello barracks. But Tony Deane seemed amiable enough and made no nasty cracks about seeing Jimmy in National Army uniform. In fact, just before they parted Tony invited Jimmy to meet him the following afternoon and gave him his address.

The next day Jimmy – in civilian clothes – called on Tony, but when the door opened and he asked for Tony Deane he was grabbed by a couple of plainclothes men and dragged inside the house. 'You want Tony Deane, do you?' said the plainclothes men, and they began to beat the hell out of poor Jimmy. He screamed his innocence saying he was a friend of Tony's, that the two of them had been comrades in the Liverpool Company, and that Tony had invited him to call around for a visit. The plainclothes men began to listen and when Jimmy told them that his brother Paddy had been killed the previous day they took their hands off him and became very sympathetic.

'Do you know what happened to Tony last night?' one of the plainclothes men asked. Jimmy didn't know of course, and then they told him that Tony was on duty at Oriel House the previous evening when someone knocked on the front door. As Tony opened the hatch in the door to see who was outside a Tommy gun was thrust through the observation hatch and Tony's head was blown off.

On returning to Mallow – which had been our company headquarters – I was surprised to learn that the company had left the town and no one seemed to know where they'd gone. I couldn't even find Jim Holloway (of Doneraile) to whom I'd given my Webley revolver for safekeeping during my absence. The revolver was the one I'd confiscated from the young Irregular I'd taken prisoner on the road from Limerick during our advance towards Kilmallock, and I'd left it with Jim before going to Liverpool because I didn't want another visitation from any would-be assassins!

Although my own company had left Mallow, they had been replaced by a new garrison of National Army troops which included a paymaster. Having returned from leave I was, of course, stony broke but when I tried to collect some back pay the paymaster refused to give me any money. Without my company, my revolver, and my pay, I hardly knew which way to turn until I happened to meet 'Tiny' Lyons who'd been with me in 'A' Company at Beggar's Bush barracks when I joined the army. Tiny Lyons and Paddy Lowe, two of the biggest men in the company, had early been promoted to corporal's rank. Paddy Lowe – God Rest him – had been killed at the time of the Four Courts fighting, but Tiny Lyons survived the worst of the Civil War and had risen to the rank of captain when I met him in Mallow.

Captain Lyons said that although he was unsure as to the whereabouts of my company, he knew that the Mechanical Transport Corps workshops in Cork urgently needed fitters and asked me to go there and help them out until I was able to rejoin my old company.

I took the next train to Cork city and when I arrived at the workshops of the Mechanical Transport Corps I was put to work almost immediately repairing Lancia armoured cars. There was such a shortage of army fitters that the Transport Corps had to hire civilian fitters, some of whom worked alongside me in both the rear axle shop and the gear box shop.

The officer in charge of the workshops had lived in Liverpool where he worked as a taxi driver. He later joined the Active Service Unit in Dublin and was a personal friend of Paddy Lawson and Vinnie Byrne – both of whom were members of Collins' Squad. The officer gave me a warm welcome saying he was glad to have a pre-Truce Volunteer in his unit.

I had no difficulty in collecting my back pay, and on my first Saturday in Cork went out in the afternoon to spend the money which was burning a hole in my pocket. By happy chance I met John O'Connell whom I hadn't seen since that Sunday afternoon (20 August 1922) when he left Mallow to accompany Michael Collins to Cork. We were delighted to meet each other again and went into the nearest pub for a quiet drink and a long chat, reminiscing about our times together in Mallow and subsequent events since we last saw each other. I was particularly anxious to get at firsthand his eyewitness account of the Beal na mBláth ambush and the death of our Commander-in-Chief.

Having discussed in detail the circumstances surrounding the tragic event, we turned to happier memories of Mallow and decided suddenly to return to Mallow that evening and renew old acquaintances. We hailed a taxi and, showing the sceptical driver that we had enough money for the fare, told him to take us to Mallow!

When we reached Mallow, John went off to visit some of his cronies while I made my way to the nurses' residence to see my girl friend. The nurses had a fit when I arrived because it was getting late in the evening, but when I produced the bottle of whiskey and a tin of fifty cigarettes I'd brought along they threw discretion to the winds and decided we should have a little party. They solved the problem of where I was to sleep that night by smuggling me into the unoccupied fever ward on the second floor of the isolation hospital. By candle-light I settled into a most comfortable bed and slept soundly until six o'clock in the morning when one of the nurses sneaked in with a mug of hot tea. In no time at all I got dressed and slipped across the fields to the far side of Mallow where I caught the early morning train back to Cork city and returned to barracks.

I hadn't been working very long in the Mechanical Transport workshops before I met Peter Horan, whose brother Mick had been with me on the night of the boarding house raids in Liverpool, and from whose home in Seaforth our party had set forth on the night I was arrested at Hall Road Station. Peter had returned to Ireland from Liverpool in order to join the National Army and was attached to a small unit known as the Railway Corps. Peter and I had a great time talking about Liverpool and the lads we both had known there.

He told me that the Railway Corps had built an armoured train which was protected with armour plating and which included an armed flatcar in front of the engine. When I learned from Peter that the train made a regular run to Killarney every weekend, I caught a ride on it the next Saturday determined to see Killarney. I'd no sooner stepped off the train in Killarney town than I met some of the lads from the Dublin Guards who had been recently commissioned as officers, and they insisted I stay with them for the weekend at the Southern Hotel where they were billeted. I spent a wonderful week-end there, enjoying the best of food at the hotel, and visiting the ruins of Muckross Abbey.

On Monday morning I rode back to Cork aboard the armoured train, but when I entered the barracks, a sergeant – an ex-British army NCO who came from Blackpool, Lancashire – told me I was under arrest for being absent without leave. The sergeant marched me up before Captain Johnny Keogh and read out the charge and then Captain Keogh dismissed him. 'All right, sergeant,' he said. 'I'll take care of this.'

As soon as the sergeant had left the room, Johnny Keogh began to grin and offering me a chair told me to sit down and have a smoke. 'How's everything in Killarney?' he asked. 'Did you see Tiny Lyons ...?' He was full of questions about the fellows we both knew and we enjoyed our chat.

Every Monday morning for the next three weeks I returned from Killarney after the weekend and each time the same sergeant charged me with being absent without leave and marched me up to Captain Keogh – with the same result. Johnny Keogh and I took advantage of the opportunity to have a friendly chat in private and regarded my 'arrest' as a joke. 'Is that poor eedjit from Lancashire still after you?' Johnny Keogh would say. 'Don't worry about the stupid bastard.'

The sergeant was furious when it finally dawned on him that the captain and I were the best of friends and were treating the Monday morning charges as a joke. 'I'll get you yet,' he'd mutter whenever we met, but I used to laugh at him.

'You'll get nothing,' I'd say to him. 'Maybe I'll get you!'

But one Monday morning when I returned after another weekend in Killarney, I was so tired that I went straight to my billet for a few hours sleep. Suddenly I was awakened to find the sergeant and five men with fixed bayonets surrounding my bed. 'Jab him if he makes a move,' said the sergeant. 'He's dangerous!'

'What the hell is this?' I asked as I sat up.

'I've got you this time,' said the sergeant. 'Get dressed and get your kit together.'

'But what's going on?' I asked him. 'What's this all about?'

'You'll find out,' he said. 'Get going.'

Jasus! I put on my uniform, packed all my gear together, and then the six of them escorted me to a lorry waiting outside the barracks. The sergeant got in beside the driver, and I piled into the back with my kit and the five soldiers with fixed bayonets, and we drove to Glanmire Station where a train was ready to pull out.

I was put into an empty compartment on the train, and while the five armed soldiers stood on the platform, the sergeant gave me a train ticket made out to Gormanston. He was sending me just about as far away as he could – to an army camp about twenty-five miles north of Dublin on the road to Drogheda! The sergeant called a porter and told him to lock the door of the train compartment.

'I got you this time,' the sergeant jeered, 'and Captain Keogh can't help you. He left Cork before you got back from Killarney.'

As the train pulled out of the station, I laughed and waved good-bye, but at the first stop which was Mallow I called a porter who unlocked the compartment and I got off the train. The opportunity for once again seeing some of my friends in Mallow was too good for me to miss. I headed straight for a shop which was owned by two brothers who invited me to stay with them for as long as I pleased. After three days in Mallow I decided to carry on for Maryborough (now Portlaoise) where I spent the night, before travelling on to Dublin. In Dublin, I stayed with the Lowes for four or five days and when the last of the little money I had was spent, I carried on for Gormanston Camp.

When I arrived at the camp I met an NCO at the gate who remembered me from Portobello barracks. He was surprised to see me again, so I told him my company had been split up and I'd been transferred to Gormanston from the Mechanical Transport Corps workshops in Cork. I didn't tell him the circumstances that led to my transfer, and he soon arranged for me to join the Command Transport depot in Gormanston Camp. He re-introduced me to another old friend of mine who was a sergeant cook, and between the two of them I began to eat and live like a king. Every weekend I got leave to go to Dublin and I was having a great time.

I liked the fellows I worked with in the transport workshops and we eventually formed a mobile crew to travel through the countryside and make emergency repairs on Lanciers which had broken down. We travelled in a Crossley tender and each of us specialised in repairing a different part of the Lancier. We almost always carried a spare rear axle with us and my job was replacing broken rear axles.

One day I met an officer in the orderly room of Gormanston Camp who, by way of introduction, said he knew my family in Co. Leitrim. He asked me where my company was and when I told him

I didn't know, he said he'd try to find out and arrange for me to rejoin them. Later in the day I met a couple of officers who'd been in the Dublin Guards, and when I asked them about Tom Flood they told me he'd been wounded. They also informed me that although the Dublin Guards were scattered throughout Kerry, many of them were in Castleisland.

That was all I wanted to know! I went straight to the transport officer and got a travel voucher for Castleisland. But I made sure I first spent a week in Dublin on the way!

When I eventually arrived in Castleisland – a lovely little village in Co. Kerry – the first person I met was Captain Tiny Lyons who took me over to the hotel where he and the other officers were billeted and there I met Seán Nolan and Eddie Flood, Tom Flood's brother. Tiny Lyons ordered a big meal for me and the four of us had a great time together. After the meal, Eddie Flood said, 'Seán, we're going to make you a sergeant, and we've got just the right job for you. We need someone to look after the quartermaster's stores.' They took me along to my new billet, handed me a bunch of keys and told me they'd give me an assistant. They also told me to be sure to come over to the hotel for a meal anytime I wanted to, but although their invitation was kindly intended, I thought I would be going too far if I took advantage of it.

With my new rank and my new job I was in clover. I had very little to do – my assistant did all the work! – and whenever a soldier came looking for a new pair of boots or a new tunic he got them without question. In fact, I had so much time on my hands that I got a little dog and spent most of the day teaching him tricks and taking him for walks.

Then one day Eddie Flood found a motor bike somewhere and brought it to me asking me to repair it and look after it for him. I soon had the motor bike running as smoothly as a sewing machine and Eddie told me I could take it out for a spin whenever I wished. I enjoyed riding around the countryside on the bike, although Eddie warned me to be careful. 'For God's sake, Seán,' he'd say, 'look out for the padjoes. The countryside around here is full of them and they might take a shot at you.'

Eventually the officers at Castleisland got a Model 'T' Ford which they used as a sort of staff car and they asked me to be their driver. They said it would be a better job than looking after the quartermaster's stores and I'd be with them wherever they went.

'But I can't drive!' I said. 'I've never driven a car in my life.'

'That's all right,' one of them said. 'We'll do the driving. We just want to have you along with us.' They knew, of course, that I was good with a gun – especially the revolver – and would be able to help them fight their way out of a tight corner if they were ever ambushed.

We had a wonderful time driving around in the car. Besides the better known towns such as Killarney and Tralee, we visited such lovely little places as Farranfore. Differences in rank were ignored on these jaunts and we called each other by our first names or nicknames.

Then one morning while I was waiting outside the hotel, an orderly came out and told me that the OC Kerry Command who'd arrived in Castleisland during the night wanted to go to Killarney immediately and that I was to drive him. Jasus! I'd never driven the damn car but I got it started and off we went.

It was a ride I'll never forget. I'll never understand how we avoided crashing through hedges, ditches and stone walls, as we skidded around the turns on those Kerry roads. We went flying through the streets of a village scattering a flock of sheep and bouncing off the sides of cattle. The OC kept muttering, 'Jesus, Mary and Joseph!' over and over again, until the shouts and screams of the terrified villagers faded behind us. 'Stop the car!' he said as soon as we were safely beyond the village. 'Get out of the driver's seat.'

Somehow I managed to stop the car and he moved in behind the steering wheel. 'How long have you been driving?' he asked.

I daren't tell him that I'd never driven a car before, so I told him that although I was the official driver, I wasn't familiar with that particular Ford motor car.

The OC drove for a while, but as the wind was making him cold, he finally suggested that perhaps all I needed was more practice in driving the car and told me to take over again. This time everything went well until just before I entered Killarney town when I almost crashed into a couple of large signposts. 'Stop it! Stop the car!' shouted the OC. 'Jasus! don't ever let me see you driving a car again!'

I finally managed to bring the car to a halt outside the hotel where the officers were billeted. The commotion of our arrival and the abrupt halt had brought the officers to the windows and front door of the hotel. When they saw that I was the unfortunate driver they all stood there bursting their sides with laughter. They knew, of course, that I really wasn't supposed to have driven the car and that the OC had been the victim of a hazardous mistake. None of them dared tell the OC that my position as a driver was merely an honorary one, because they didn't want to get Eddie Flood, Tiny Lyons and the other officers into trouble.

The OC had already left Killarney town by the time I reported for duty the next morning and I caught a ride back to Castleisland with someone else. I told Eddie Flood what had happened and that I was afraid there might be repercussions from the wild ride I'd given the OC. 'Ah, Seán,' he said, 'never mind that Kerry bastard. He's a bit peculiar. He's not at all sociable.'

I never heard any more about the ride to Killarney. When the OC saw the welcome I got from the officers at the hotel who knew me, he must have realised I was one of the old crowd and let the matter drop.

Our relatively uneventful routine at Castleisland was suddenly shattered by the tragic news that a nurse had been murdered at Scartaglin – about five miles or so from Castleisland – by one of our lieutenants. Both the officers and men at Castleisland were terribly upset by the tragedy. We all knew the lieutenant quite well; he had been a good man but the poor fellow, God help him, had become too fond of his drink. We didn't know whether or not the terrible strain of the Tan War and then the Civil War had become unbearable for him, but he drank heavily. Quite often when he took us out of Mallow on a march he'd halt the column for a rest while he stepped to the side of the road to take a swig from a bottle of whiskey which he always carried. The lads in the company got upset when they saw him drinking like that, because he'd be worse than useless to us as an officer if we were ambushed. We had the greatest respect for him on account of his reputation for courage, but we didn't want our lives thrown away if we were suddenly attacked and he was too drunk to command us properly. Eventually he was moved to another unit and ended up in Castleisland. When he shot the nurse whom he'd been courting, the army decided he had to be punished and he was hanged at Mountjoy Prison.

Some time after the tragedy at Scartaglin, Eddie Flood and Tiny Lyons told me that I was being transferred from Castleisland to Ballymun barracks. Command Headquarters at Tralee had ordered that the security of prisoners held in the prison adjacent to the military barracks be supervised by four NCOs specially selected for their integrity and for their loyalty to the army. And that was how I found myself chosen for the thankless job at Ballymun barracks. Five Irregulars had been executed there prior to my arrival, and the place had already earned a bad reputation for the treatment of its prisoners.

Of all the counties in Ireland Kerry was probably the most determined in its opposition to the Treaty and the authority of the National Army and it was from Kerry as well as from parts of West Cork that the Irregulars drew their greatest support. Most of the prisoners held at Ballymun were anti-Treatyites who'd either been captured in the field or arrested in their homes, but the great majority of them could be better described as political prisoners than as prisoners of war.

The bulk of the prisoners were housed in four wings of the barracks' prison, each of which was placed under the general supervision of an army NCO. The four of us NCOs had our own small mess where we lived like kings with a couple of prisoners who acted as our batmen. We had little direct contact with the rest of the prisoners who ranged freely in the wings. Many of them had knocked holes through the walls of adjoining cells despite the fact that all the locks had been smashed off the doors. The prisoners spent most of each day drinking tea and chatting with each other, and at night time the Kerrymen often held their own ceilís.

One of our duties was to supervise the visits between prisoners and their relatives or close friends. The prisoner met his visitor in a room set aside for such visits and both parties sat facing each other from the opposite ends of a table. I could hardly bear to be present when a man was being visited by his wife or fiancee. It was a heartbreaking experience.

In addition to the political prisoners there were also a few civilians who were imprisoned for minor criminal offences. At that time there was no effective civil police force available to maintain law and order in the area, so if a 'bad actor' was reported to our CO a couple of soldiers arrested the offender and threw him into prison. If a priest, for example, complained that a woman in his parish had been beaten up by her drunken husband, a couple of soldiers were sent to take the man and put him in prison for a couple of weeks.

Among the civilian prisoners there were only four women, each of whom had committed some petty offence. One of them called Gussie had stolen a lady's handbag. Another woman was imprisoned because she'd earned a bad reputation for running about with married men.

The barracks' prison was surrounded by two walls: an outer wall and an inner wall. The inner wall was guarded by a party of soldiers about half a company strong who were relieved each week by a fresh party of soldiers. The outer or main gates of the prison were guarded solely by military police.

At the entrance to the wings of the prison there was a small section for soldiers of the National Army who'd been court-martialled for various military offences. The military prisoners were totally isolated from all other prisoners and were under the exclusive control of the small detachment of military police. Of all the inmates, I felt sorriest for the military prisoners because they were regularly beaten up by the military police who were hated so much – not only by the prisoners but by almost everyone in the National Army – that they never dared to go out of the barracks alone. It seemed as if they had been recruited from among the cruellest swine in all Ireland, and the man universally blamed for their excesses was General Paddy Daly.

When I first met him at Beggar's Bush barracks, Paddy Daly was one of the most admired heroes of the IRA because of his work in Collins' Squad. But probably as a result of the terrible strain of fighting the Black and Tans and then the Irregulars, he turned into one of the most hated officers of the National Army, and his name was cursed throughout the length and breadth of Ireland.

A lieutenant and his wife (who was a nurse) were permanently in charge of the prison barracks, but not once in all the time I was there, did I ever see either of them inspect or visit the prison. As outraged as I was by the suffering endured by the military prisoners, there was nothing either I or the other NCOs could do to stop it. In their attempt to 'professionalise' the Irish army, the new caste of army officers – who were rapidly succumbing to the lure of an alien class consciousness – had stifled the Volunteer spirit and replaced it with a harsh and brutal discipline that even included flogging. Such a system would have inflicted its severest retribution for any protest I might have made. I could see that the only option I had was to take my release from the army and distance myself from the shame of what was happening at Ballymun, so I took my discharge from the army on 15 February 1924.

Postscript

Shortly after his discharge from the army in 1924, John Pinkman was employed as a fitter on the construction of the Shannon hydro-electric scheme at Ardnacrusha, Co. Limerick, but disillusioned with post-Civil War Ireland, he began a 30-year 'voyaging' by working his passage aboard a British freighter to America. Landing illegally in Boston where he 'jumped ship', he made his way to New York where he married his childhood sweetheart Annie Rooney (from Glenade, Co. Leitrim) in 1929. He 'rode the rods' across the United States as a hobo during the Depression, but began a seafaring career when he obtained a position as a marine engineer aboard a cruise ship sailing out of New York on the South American route.

He sailed on a variety of ships that took him through the turbulent events of the 1930s, 1940s and 1950s, and his ports of call were often exotic and sometimes dangerous. During the Second World War he survived the Battle of the Atlantic and the convoys to Russia, North Africa and the Far East. After the Second World War, he returned to the United States legally and fished commercially off the coast of California until he became homesick for Ireland so he returned in 1955. Employed as an engineering fitter at the Liffey Dockyards and then for the Board of Works at Dun Laoghaire, he was forced to retire after his first heart attack. He was last employed as a night watchman for Dublin Corporation until he retired to St Patrick's Home, Kilmainham where he suffered his fourth and final heart attack on 26 March 1970 and died. He was buried in Glasnevin Cemetery where a detachment from McKee barracks, Eastern Command, provided military honours at his funeral.

He was predeceased by his wife Anne Bridget (Rooney) who died in 1965 at Ballyshannon, Co. Donegal.

Notes

1 *Mag Uidhir: anglice,* Maguire, 'descendant of the ruddy-complexioned man.' *Uidhir*, gen. case of *odhar,* an indeterminate colour or complexion – dun, tanned, etc.

2 *Ó Gormfhlaithigh: anglice*, O'Gormley, 'descendant of the blue warrior-prince.'

3 *Sinn Féin:* 'by ourselves alone,' a political movement which grew out of the amalgamation (during the first decade of the 1900s) of several separatist societies. Owing its inspiration to Arthur Griffith, its policy was to achieve the 'national self-development' of Ireland.

4 Irish Republican Brotherhood: a secret society formed in Dublin on 17 March 1858 by James Stephens for the purpose of 'the overthrowing of British power in Ireland and establishing an independent Republic.' Reorganised in 1873, its Supreme Council planned the Rising of 1916.

5 Cumann na mBan: a women's auxiliary formed in 1913 and affiliated to the Irish Volunteers.

6 *An tÓglach,* ('The Volunteer'), Vol. 2, No. 2, Winter, 1967, Old IRA Publications, Dublin.

7 *Ibid.*, p. 2.

8 Royal Irish Constabulary: originally formed as the Irish Constabulary by Robert Peel in 1836, Queen Victoria granted them the title of 'Royal' for suppressing the Fenian outbreaks of 1856-67. A paramilitary police force normally 11,000 strong, they served as 'the eyes and ears' of the British administration. They were formally disbanded in August, 1922.

9 Active Service Unit: a body of fifty full-time Volunteers from the Dublin Brigade. Formed in January, 1920, and paid £4.10.0 per week, their function was to provide support for Michael Collins' Squad. They openly fought British forces in the streets of Dublin.

10 Black and Tans: a para-military police force recruited in England from among unemployed British ex-servicemen and ticket-of-leave convicts to supplement the Royal Irish Constabulary. Paid ten shillings per day and nicknamed Black and Tans because they were originally uniformed in khaki tunics and black trousers, the first contingent

arrived in Ireland on 25 March, 1920, 'to make Ireland hell for the rebels'.

11 Reign of Terror: the most vicious period during Ireland's War of Independence and raged from August to October, 1920. It was a direct result of Hamar Greenwood's (Chief Secretary for Ireland) Bill for the Restoration of Order in Ireland which came into effect on 2 August 1920, and gave enlarged powers to the military and to the Black and Tans. The Reign of Terror was particularly ruthless in Co. Galway and the West of Ireland generally.

12 Cathal Brugha: Minister of Defense in the First Dáil (during the summer of 1920).

13 Terence MacSwiney: Lord Mayor of Cork, arrested 12 August 1920, and sentenced to two years penal servitude for possessing 'seditious documents.' He died in Brixton Prison 25 October 1920, having been on hunger strike for seventy-four days.

14 Jack (John) Plunkett: the youngest of Count George Plunkett's three sons, each of whom participated in the Rising of 1916. Jack Plunkett's brother, Joseph Mary, a member of the Military Council of the IRB and a signatory of the Proclamation, was executed for his part in the Rising on 4 May 1916, at Kilmainham Jail.

15 Professor Michael Hayes: Minister of Education in the First Dáil. His home was at No 49 Longwood Avenue (between Portobello barracks and Wellington barracks).

16 *The Times,* London, Monday, 29 November 1920, p.14.

17 *The Times, ibid.*

18 O'Donovan Rossa: *Diarmuid* (*anglice,* Jeremiah) O'Donovan (1831–1915), of Roscarberry, Co. Cork. Sentenced to life imprisonment in 1865 for his activities aimed at ridding Ireland of the British by 'Dynamite, Greek fire, or Hell fire if it could be had', he was released from prison in 1871 and emigrated to America where he became an energetic organiser of Fenianism. He died in Staten Island, New York and was buried in Glasnevin Cemetery, Dublin on 1 August, 1915. Patrick Pearse, in his funeral oration at the graveside, hinted at the Rising which took place the following year.

19 Processions: to commemorate the death and funeral of Terence MacSwiney, Lord Mayor of Cork. Between nine and ten thousand people took part in each of the two processions.

20 Henry Maden (1892–1960): Called to Bar, Middle Temple 1916; Liberal M.P. for Lonsdale 1923–24. He died 17 November 1960.

21 George Justin Lynskey (Ir. *Ó Loinscigh),* 1888–1957: Educated at St Francis Xavier College, Liverpool and Liverpool University LLB 1907, LLM 1908. Admitted a solicitor 1910, called to Bar, Inner Temple 1920, KC 1930, Bencher, Inner Temple 1938, Judge of Salford Hundred Court of Record 1938-44. Knighted 1944. He was the first solicitor in modern English legal history to become a chief justice. The second solicitor to do so was Lord Widgery who conducted the enquiry into the shooting of 13 Civil Rights demonstrators by British paratroops in Derry on 30 January 1972.

22 Gordon Hewart (1870–1943), 1st Viscount Bury: Called to Bar, Inner Temple 1902, Solicitor General in Lloyd George's cabinet, December, 1916, and one of the signatories of the Anglo-Irish Treaty, 1921.

23 Edward George Hemmerde, 1871-1948. Called to Bar, Inner Temple 1897, KC 1908, Recorder of Liverpool 1909. Liberal MP for East Denbighshire 1906–10, and for N.W. Norfolk 1912–18 before joining the Labour Party and becoming Labour MP for Crewe Division (of Cheshire) 1922–24

24 The White Cross Association: a non-partisan organisation established in the US at De Valera's instigation during his fund-raising campaign there in 1919. The purpose of the White Cross was to relieve distress in Ireland during the War of Independence. It also provided aid to Irish prisoners.

25 Canon Edward St John, chaplain at Walton Prison, 1913–25; died at Twyford Abbey Nursing Home, London on 11 June 1934 and was buried at Mortlake, Surrey.

26 Evidently the mutiny still rankles the British military establishment. Lieut Gen. Alan Shepperd (Retd), Senior Librarian of the Royal Military Academy, Sandhurst, in his book *The Connaught Rangers* (Men-at-Arms Series, Osprey Publishing Ltd., Reading, 1972) devotes only three lines to it. For a more complete history of the regiment – including a detailed account of the mutiny and the brutal punishment inflicted on the mutineers – read T. P. Kilfeather's *The Connaught Rangers,* Anvil Books, Tralee, 1969.

27 Sir Rigby Philip Watson Swift (1874–1937): His legal practice was chiefly in criminal and licencing work, and when appointed to the King's

Bench division of the High Court (and knighted) in June, 1920 he was, at the age of 46 years, the youngest judge on the bench. During 1921 he presided over the trials of a total of 17 IRA Volunteers charged with treason and felony. He died 18 October 1937.

28 Frederick E. Smith, 1st Earl Birkenhead, 1872–1930: Called to Bar, Gray's Inn 1899, MP for Walton 1906. Offered Lord Chancellorship and elevated to peerage as Viscount Birkenhead, 1919. F. E. Smith, an avowed opponent of Home Rule and Irish nationalists, was Sir Edward Carson's principal aide during the resistance to Home Rule organised in Ulster in 1914. Solicitor General in 1915, he succeeded Carson as Attorney General in November 1915, and personally led the prosecution at the trial of Sir Roger Casement. He was one of the signatories to the Anglo-Irish Treaty, 1921.

29 Translation: 'Be merciful to the conquered' (Virgil, *The Aeneid*, Book *VI*, l. 853).

30 Francis George Morgan, Capt., South Wales Borderers, appointed governor of H. M. Prison, Dartmoor, 1921.

31 Hon. Edward Fleming French, Maj., Cheshire Regiment, appointed deputy-governor of H. M. Prison, Dartmoor, 1921.

32 Field Marshal Viscount French who replaced Lord Wimborne as Lord Lieutenant of Ireland in May, 1918. Michael Collins personally planned the ambush of Viscount French which took place at Ashtown Cross (north of Dublin) on 19 December 1919 because French was so largely responsible for directing the campaign against the IRA. Viscount French survived the ambush, but was recalled and replaced by Lord Fitzallen on 1 April 1921.

33 For an account of the treament meted out to a group of Fenians sentenced in 1883 to life imprisonment, read Thomas J. Clarke's *Glimpses of an Irish Felon's Prison Life,* 1922.

34 Fr Bernard Leo Finnegan was *not* from Co. Cavan! Born in 1876 in Loughgilly, Co. Armagh where his family had lived for several generations, he completed his religious studies at Carlow College and was ordained in 1902. 'Affiliated' to the Diocese of Plymouth, he was appointed Catholic chaplain to Dartmoor Prison, 1910–17, and again from when it reopened until he retired from Prison Service in 1931. He died 27 November 1955.

35 Apparently a ruse. The journals of nearby Buckfast Abbey, which would have recorded such a mediation by one of its monks had it occurred, contain no reference to the event.

36 Bryan MacNeill: son of Eoin MacNeill, then Minister of Education in the Provisional Government of the Irish Free State.

37 *An Cuilfhionn* ('the maid with the fair, flowing locks').

38 Countess Markievicz: Constance Georgina Gore-Booth, born 4 February 1868, at Lisadell, County Sligo, she married Count Casimir Markievicz in 1900. Founder of Fianna Éireann, she was second in command (under Michael Mallin) of the Irish Citizen Army contingent at St Stephen's Green during the Rising of 1916.

39 Flying columns: mobile IRA units of up to 100 men adopting the hit-and-run tactics of Boer commandoes.

40 Auxilaries: Auxiliary Division of the RIC, widely known in Ireland as the 'Auxies'. Formed at the suggestion of Winston Churchill and recruited from among unemployed ex-officers of the British army, they comprised a force of approximately 1,500 men and were placed under the command of Brig.-Gen. F. P. Crozier. They were responsible for many of the worst atrocities of the Tan War.

41 Captain Paddy Daly: Eventually promoted to the rank of general. Not to be confused with the young medical student of the same name who, after the arrest of Neill Kerr and Stephen Lanigan, became one of Michael Collins' most trusted agents in England.

42 US President J. F. Kennedy was so impressed by the Irish military funeral drill performed at the Arbour Hill memorial service (on 28 June 1963) during his visit to Ireland, that when Jackie Kennedy requested the same contingent of Irish army officer cadets to perform the drill at the President's funeral in Arlington National Cemetery on 25 November 1963 the Irish government readily complied.

43 Calton Younger, *Ireland's Civil War* (London: Frederick Muller Ltd., 1968), pp. 275–280.

44 Eoin Neeson, *The Civil War in Ireland* (Cork: The Mercier Press, 1966), p. 61.

45 *Ibid.*

46 Younger, *op. cit.*, p. 277.

47 Neill (senior) intended to join his three sons in the Kimmage Garrison, but the messenger sent by Michael Collins to give Neill the exact date of the Rising delayed his departure in order to attend the Fairyhouse races on Easter Monday afternoon – unaware of the nature and urgency of the message he was carrying. When Neill finally received the message, the Rising had already begun.

48 Seán Lemass (Taoiseach, 1959–66) died on 11 May 1971 at the age of 71 years.

49 Oriel House: headquarters of the Irish Free State's Special Branch of detectives. A large house (No. 36) in Westland Row, it later became the home of the Royal Irish Academy of Music.

50 Suffering from battle hysteria, Commandant de Valera had to be forcibly restrained by some of his men of the Boland's Mill garrison before the end of the Easter Week's fighting and removed to Sir Patrick Dun's Hospital. It was in a room of the hospital that De Valera made his formal surrender to Captain Hitzen of the 5th Lincolnshire Regiment at about 1.00pm on Sunday, 30 April 1916.

51 The building (No. 43 O'Connell Street) was subsequently rebuilt and occupied by Boylan's Shoe Store. The adjacent building (No. 44) later became the home of TWA's Dublin office.

52 'Peter-the-Painter': Luger P. 08 9mm Parabellum – a highly regarded German automatic pistol.

53 Dorothy Macardle, *The Irish Republic* (Dublin: Irish Press Ltd., 1951).

54 The executive of an army convention (sponsored by IRA officers opposed to the Treaty) that met in the Mansion House, Dublin, on 26 March 1922, appointed Liam Lynch its Chief-of-Staff. Reappointed Chief-of-Staff by the convention's executive when the convention reassembled on 9 April, Lynch was rejected when the convention, which met for the third time on 18 June, split over Tom Barry's motion to resume the war against the British.

55 The decision had actually been made on the night of 12 July but not announced until the next day.

56 Eoin Neeson, *The Civil War in Ireland* (Cork: The Mercier Press, 1966), pp. 133–139.

57 Volunteers Bolster and Willis were instrumental in both the planning and the attack on Mallow barracks by Cork No. 2 (North) Brigade on 28 September 1920 – the only British military barracks captured by the IRA in the Tan War.

58 Frank Flood: hanged with five other Volunteers (including Paddy Moran and Thomas Whelan) in Mountjoy Prison on the morning of 14

March 1921.

59 Colonel James C. Fitzmaurice died in Dublin on 26 September 1965 at the age of 68 years.

60 Rex Taylor, *Michael Collins* (London: Hutchinson & Co. Ltd., 1958).

61 Calton Younger, *Ireland's Civil War* (London: Frederick Muller Ltd., 1968), p. 420.

Acknowledgements

I am deeply grateful to the many individuals who provided me with corroborative information and materials concerning events referred to in this book. Several of those who so generously assisted me in substantiating and verifying the author's accounts were themselves participants in or, at least, observers of the events described. It is readily acknowledged that not all those who assisted me shared John Pinkman's convictions or his allegiances, particularly in relation to the Anglo-Irish Treaty of 1921 and the subsequent Civil War in Ireland, but their assistance was, nevertheless, invaluable in confirming the author's record. The opinions and interpretations of the author are, of course, his own.

I have respected the anonymity of the few individuals who requested that their identities not be revealed. Those whose assistance I am happy and proud to acknowledge include: General Seán MacEoin; General Richard Mulcahy; Eamon de Valera, Uachtarán; Captain Liam McNeive, last surviving pre-1916 officer of the Liverpool Company, Irish Volunteers; Lieut-Col Paddy Daly, Senior Physician, St Bricin's Military Hospital; Professor Liam Ó Briain; Tom Kerr, Ned Lane, Paddy Caldwell, Seamus Monaghan, Bernie Meehan, Dudley O'Carroll, Joe Duffy, Óglaigh na hÉireann; Annie Curran, granddaughter of John Philpot Curran, and Treasurer of Branch No. 13, Irish Self-Determination League of Great Britain, Liverpool; Mrs R. McNance, Liverpool Cumann na mBan; Roisin Finn, daughter of Maura Mackey, Liverpool Cumann na mBan and member of the Four Courts garrison; Rev. Bro. John P. Flood, FMS, brother of Cmdt Tom Flood; Nora Thornton, sister of Frank Thornton, captain in pre-1916 Irish Volunteers, Liverpool and one of Michael Collins' principal intelligence officers during the War of Independence; Pádraig Thornton, son of Frank Thornton; Frances Geraghty and Mary Cunningham, sisters of John Pinkman, Liverpool; Margaret and Mary Alice Pinkman, cousins of John Pinkman, Co. Leitrim.

My sincere thanks are also due to: Rev Fr F. X. Martin, OSA,

University College, Dublin; Captain Liam Ó Ceallaigh, Personal Staff Officer to the Adjutant General, Army HQ, Dublin; Gerard Slevin, Chief Herald of Ireland; Rev. Seán Corkery, Libararian, St Patrick's College, Maynooth; Dr T. F. Elliot, Col and Director, Army Medical Corps, Army HQ, Dublin; Prionsias Mac Aonghusa, political commentator and journalist, Dublin; Tim Pat Coogan, editor *Irish Press,* Dublin; Canon M. Kearney, PP, St Mary's, Carrick-on-Shannon; Director and staff, National Library of Ireland, Kildare Street, Dublin; Librarian and staff, City of Dublin Libraries, Pearse Street Branch, Dublin; Director and staff, Ordnance Survey Office, Map Stores Branch, Phoenix Park, Dublin; Registrar-General and staff, Office of the Registrar-General Custom House, Dublin; Fr R. Atherton, Chaplain, H. M. Prison, Walton, Liverpool; R. Sharpe France, Co. Archivist, Lancashire Record Office, Sessions House, Preston, Lancs.; L. J. L. Hill, General Sales Manager, Webley & Scott Ltd, Birmingham; Photographic Section, Bord Failte Éireann, Dublin; Ian Finlay, Photographer, Booterstown, Dublin; Douglas Kearon, photographer, Waterloo, Liverpool; Mr & Mrs St Leger, residents, Findlater Building, Dublin; Sr Mary Paul, Mother Superior and Sr Lucienne, Little Sisters of the Poor, Kilmainham, Dublin; Sr Paschal, St Vincent de Paul Hospital, Dublin; Adjutant, Eastern Command, McKee barracks, Dublin.

FEM

More Interesting Books

Michael Collins
and the Making of the Irish State

Edited by Gabriel Doherty and Dermot Keogh

Michael Collins was one of the most important leaders of his or any other age in Irish history. His contribution to the founding of the Irish state was immense even by the standards of a talented generation which included politicians of the calibre of Eamon de Valera, Arthur Griffith, Willam T. Cosgrave, Richard Mulcahy, Kevin O'Higgins, Patrick McGilligan, Harry Boland, Seán Lemass, Frank Aiken and Seán MacEntee.

Collins has generally been portrayed in writing and film as a revoloutionary man of action, a guerrilla leader, a military tactician and a figure of great personal charm, courage and ingenuity. He was in fact a man of many parts.These essays illustrate the multifaceted and complex character that was Michael Collins.

This book is a professional evaluation of Michael Collins and his contribution to the making of the Irish state. With contributions from many of the leading historians working in the field, and written in an accessible style, the essays make full use of archival material and provide new findings and insights into the life and times of Michael Collins.

The contributors examine Collins as Minister for Finance, his role in intelligence, his policy towards the north, his career as Commander-in-Chief, the origins of the Civil War, his relationship with De Valera and how academics view his place in Irish history.

The collection also includes two personal memoirs by Fr Gearóid O'Sullivan and Margot Gearty on Collins and the Kiernans of Granard, County Longford. Both shed new light on Kitty and on her remarkable sisters.

Michael Collins
The Man Who Won the War

T. Ryle Dwyer

In formally proposing the adoption of the Anglo-Irish Treaty on 19 December 1921 Arthur Griffith referred to Michael Collins as 'the man who won the War', much to the annoyance of the Defence Minister Cathal Brugha, who questioned whether Collins 'had ever fired a shot at any enemy of Ireland'.

Who was this Michael Collins, and what was his real role in the War of Independence? How was it that two sincere, selfless individuals like Griffith and Brugha, could differ so strongly about him?

This is the story of a charismatic rebel who undermined British morale and inspired Irish people with exploits, both real and imaginary. He co-ordinated the sweeping Sinn Féin election victory of 1918, organised the IRA, set up the first modern intelligence network, masterminded a series of prison escapes and supervised the fundraising to finance the movement.

Collins probably never killed anybody himself, but he did order the deaths of people standing in his way, and even advocated kidnapping an American President. He was the prototype of the urban terrorist and the real architect of the Black and Tan War.

The Path to Freedom

Michael Collins

Many books have been written about the life and death of Michael Collins. *The Path to Freedom* is the only book he wrote himself.

These articles and speeches, first published in 1922, throw light not only on the War of Independence, the Civil War and the foundation of the Free State but on crucial contemporary issues.

> The actions taken indicated an over-keen desire for peace, and although terms of truce were virtually agreed upon, they were abandoned because the British leaders thought their actions indicated weakness, and they consequently decided to insist upon the surrender of our arms. The result was the continuance of the struggle.

Michael Collins on efforts to bring about a truce earlier in 1920.

The Course of Irish History

Edited by T. W. Moody and F. X. Martin

This book provides a rapid short survey, with geographical introduction, of the whole course of Ireland's history. Based on a series of television programmes, it is designed to be both popular and authoritative, concise but comprehensive, highly selective but balanced and fair-minded, critical but constructive and sympathetic. A distinctive feature is its wealth of illustrations.

The present edition is a revised and enlarged version of the original book. New material has been added, bringing the narrative to the IRA ceasefire of 31 August 1994.

The SAS in Ireland

Raymond Murray

The SAS in Ireland traces the history of the British Army Special Air Services Regiment, the SAS, in Ireland over the past twenty years. It details their activities – intelligence gathering and surveillance, their links with British Intelligence, notably MI5 and MI6, their connection with sectarian murders and many other deaths.

Fr Raymond Murray is a respected commentator on events in the north of Ireland. In this book he analyses in detail the activities of the SAS and plain clothes soldiers in the six counties. His research leads him to the conclusion that in many instances the SAS engaged in a careful and organised shoot-to-kill policy.

Hard Time
Armagh Gaol 1971–86

Raymond Murray

Raymond Murray was Catholic chaplain of Armagh Women's Gaol from 1971 to 1986. The number of women political prisoners increased from two in 1971 to more than one hundred in the 1972–76 period. Thirty-two of these women were imprisoned without trial. Most of the political prisoners in gaol were girls in their teenage years and one internee was in her sixties. In the 1972–76 period the prisoners had 'special category' or 'political' status.

Raymond Murray's reports became more hard-hitting as injustices increased and oppression grew. Some prisoners in Armagh Gaol alleged beatings by male officers, strip-searches, denial of access to toilets, denial of laundry, denial of visits from concerned persons, the use of 23-hour lock-up and other degrading practices.